THE MAKING OF BRITAIN

The Age of Revolution

THE MAKING OF BRITAIN

The Age of Revolution

edited by
Lesley M. Smith

**MACMILLAN
EDUCATION**

First published 1987

Published by
MACMILLAN EDUCATION LTD
Houndmills, Basingstoke, Hampshire RG21 2XS
and London
Companies and representatives
throughout the world

Typeset and designed by Columns of Reading

Printed in Great Britain by
R. J. Acford, Chichester

British Library Cataloguing in Publication Data
The Age of revolution.—(The Making of
Britain)—(A Channel Four book)
1. Great Britain—History—18th century
2. Great Britain—History—19th century
I. Smith, Lesley M.   II. Series   III. Series
941   DA480
ISBN 0-333-43866-3
ISBN 0-333-43867-1 Pbk

Contents

List of Illustrations   vii

Acknowledgements   x

Preface   xi

Introduction   1
Lesley M. Smith

1   The Echo of the Tumbril   9
Michael Broers

2   A Question of Machinery   23
Maxine Berg

3   From Retribution to Reform   37
Boyd Hilton

4   The New Babylons   49
Penelope J. Corfield

5   The Working Classroom   63
Philip Gardner

6   'Domestic Harmony, Public Virtue'   75
Catherine Hall

7   The Victorian State: Order or Liberty?   89
V. A. C. Gatrell

8   A Union without Unity   103
Roy Foster

9   The View from the Colonies   117
     David Dabydeen

10   A Week at the Seaside   131
     James Walvin

11   The Leap in the Dark   145
     Michael Bentley

12   The Invention of the Past   159
     Peter J. Bowler

     Notes   173

     Notes on Contributors   187

     Index   191

List of Illustrations

Chapter 1

1. *The Black Watch at Bushy Run*, a painting by C. W. Geffreys   10
2. The surrender of Lord Cornwallis during the
   American War of Independence   13
3. The execution of Louis XVI   15
4. *The Coronation of Napoleon 1804*, by David   17
5. The 'wooden walls' of the Royal Navy   17
6. *Little Boney* by Gillray   21

Chapter 2

1. *Science Making Giant Strides*, by George Cruickshank   23
2. The spinning jenny   27
3. A calico-printing workshop   29
4. Wensleydale knitters by George Walker (from
   The Costume History of Yorkshire, 1814)   33
5. Industrial unrest: an attack on the flying shuttle   34
6. Industrial unrest: a factory destroyed   35

Chapter 3

1. The nineteenth-century view of Heaven   37
2. The altar piece of All Saints Church, Margaret Street,
   London; Christ on the cross   40
3. Christ in Majesty   40
4. Victorian Christmas celebrations   41
5. *A Summer Day in Hyde Park*, by John Ritchie (1858)   45
6. The achievements of British industry: the
   Crystal Palace Exhibition Hall   46

Chapter 4

1. *The Tower of Babel*, by Breughel   50
2. *Gin Lane*, by Hogarth   52
3. *Beer Street*, by Hogarth   52
4. The Royal Exchange in the late eighteenth century   54
5. The stage coach to Town   56
6. A nineteenth-century panorama of Manchester   60

Chapter 5

1. Four Pope's Parade, Bristol   63
2. Slum dwellings, Bluegate Fields, London   65
3. Private Venture Schools   69
4. Private Venture Schools   69
5. Private Venture Schools   69
6. 1851 Census return for Bristol   72

Chapter 6

1. Queen Caroline   76
2. The trial of Queen Caroline, 1820   77
3. Hannah Moore   80
4. A warehouse in Great Charles Street, Birmingham   83
5. James Luckcock   84
6. Hancock's Jewellery Shop, Birmingham   84
7. A typical house in Hagley Road, Edgbaston   85

Chapter 7

1. Three prisoners at Derby Gaol   90
2. A City of London policeman   92
3. Cheshire police on duty in Yorkshire during the
   1893 miners' strike   93
4. Manchester detectives, 1890   94
5. Bristol police performing cutlass drill   97
6. The Portsmouth police force, 1865   99

Chapter 8

1. The murder of a drummer boy by rebels in 1798   106
2. Daniel O'Connell's house, Derrymane, County Kerry   109
3. O'Connell addressing a meeting at Trim   109
4. Attack on a potato store   111
5. A weekly meeting of the Repeal Association   112
6. An eviction in southern Ireland   113

Chapter 9

1.   The transportation of prisoners to Australia   118
2.   Liverpool in the seventeenth century   121
3.   Liverpool: a bustling port by 1840   122
4.   The British take the railway to India:
     Sursuttee Bridge and Aqueduct   124
5.   Bones of mutineers in a courtyard at Lucknow   125
6.   The hanging of defeated mutineers   126
7.   Portrait of Olaudah Equiano   128

Chapter 10

1.   A football match   133
2.   Promenading at Bath   135
3.   The Pump Room at Bath   137
4.   The beginnings of seaside development at Brighton 138
5.   The new fashion for swimming   140
6.   Cremone Gardens, 1864   142

Chapter 11

1.   William Ewart Gladstone   146
2.   Benjamin Disraeli, Earl of Beaconsfield   146
3.   Banquet in the Guildhall, London, to celebrate
     the passing of the 1832 Reform Act   147
4.   The Tory idealised view of a farmer   150
5.   An election in the 1850s   151
6.   Lord John Russell   152
7.   *The Political Tailors*, a *Punch* cartoon of 1867 153

Chapter 12

1.   Two models of cultural evolution   161
2.   New classifications for prehistory   164
3.   The Megalosaurus, Crystal Palace   165
4.   William Buckland lecturing in Oxford   166
5.   *HMS Beagle*   168
6.   The empire at work   170

Acknowledgements

The editor and publishers wish to thank the following who have kindly given permission for the use of illustrations:

Her Majesty the Queen; Victoria Art Gallery, Bath City Council; Avon and Somerset Constabulary; the Black Watch Royal Highlands Regiment; Mary Evans Picture Library; The Royal College of Surgeons of England; The Illustrated London News Picture Library; Greater Manchester Police; Exeter City Museums; Photographie Giraudon; Kunsthistorisches Museum, Vienna; The Museum of the History of Science, Oxford University; the Trustees of the British Museum; The British Library; Yale University Art Gallery; Portsmouth City Museum and Art Gallery; Reference Library Department, Birmingham Public Libraries; Natonal Maritime Museum, Greenwich; Lincolnshire Constabulary; Bridgeman Art Library; E.T. Archive; National Portrait Gallery; Mansell Collection; Museum of London; All Saints Church, W1; BBC Hulton Picture Library; East Sussex County Library; National Library of Ireland, Dublin.

Preface

This volume accompanies the fourth series of the London Weekend/ Channel Four study of British history, *The Making of Britain*. I should like to thank those at London Weekend Television involved in the production of the series, Jane Hewland and, in particular, Trevor Phillips, for the help they have given me in shaping this book. My thanks are due also to the contributors whose interest and commitment to this series has made my task very much easier and also very pleasurable. Several other scholars have generously shared their interpretations of the eighteenth and nineteenth centuries with me and I should like to thank Michael Anderson, J. W. Burrow, Kenneth Hudson, Christine MacCleod, Alan O'Day, Linda Pollock, Andrew Porter, Raphael Samuel, Gareth Steadman Jones and Stephen Yeo for taking the time to talk to me about this series. Linda Stradling has accomplished the picture research for the book and the series with great skill while Pam Wilkinson's help in typing a difficult manuscript and teaching me to use a word processor has been inestimable. Vanessa Couchman and Michael Jupe have again proved most patient editors. Finally, I should like to thank Steven Davis, whose patience, good humour and support has ensured that my work on this book and series has never become too onerous.

L.M.S.
London, June 1986

Introduction

In February 1958, the Victorian Society was founded in London. In its early years, with a nucleus of only some three hundred members, the society pledged itself to the preservation of the architectural heritage of Britain's industrial past. At the time, both public policy and private taste disdained anything Victorian. The prosperity of the post-war years engendered a belief in all sectors of society that it would be possible to build a new and much better society on the ruins of the old. New societies required new symbols and planners and developers, ironically building on a Victorian tradition of philanthropic improvement in the living and working conditions of the anonymous masses, began to transform their ideal future of equality and opportunity into reality. The suburbs and the factories, the High Streets and the terraced houses of the nineteenth century lay at the mercy of any visionary local authority with a blue-print for the future and cash-in-hand, and in the process of building this new utopia, they began to destroy the housing, the public buildings and the very heart of Victorian cities and towns all over Britain.

Thus when the Victorian society was founded, interest in Victorian architecture was limited only to the speed with which it could be destroyed, while any appreciation of Victorian taste signalled affected eccentricity. If the past was appreciated, it was for the elegant proportions of Georgian buildings, which were far more in tune with the economical, modernist taste of the 1950s and 1960s. The Gothic Victorian interior, overcrowded with pictures and ornament, was also rejected by an avidly consumerist society entranced by the sparse lines and pale woods of Scandinavian furniture, and its own ability to choose the furnishings for its homes as fashion, not tradition, dictated.

Even more important in the disparagement of Victorian taste was the fact that many people (or their parents) had grown to adulthood in Victorian slums, studied in dark Victorian schools, laboured in Victorian factories, in cities and towns largely created by Victorian entrepreneurs' searches for profit. This was a past associated with poverty and inequality from which the high wages and the new homes of post-war Britain offered an escape.

The same was true of that view of life popularly accepted as Victorian: the constraints of a puritan morality; the blind attachment to King and Country that had taken Britain into two lengthy and bloody wars; the notion that Britain had a superior role in guiding the destiny of the world. From the vantage point of the 1950s and 1960s, the Victorian era represented all that the twentieth century, come of age after the Second World War, had finally jettisoned.

But just as the Victorians themselves became interested in their past at a time of very rapid change in their working lives and their physical environment – in their case, caused by the industrial revolution – our society, too, has begun to appreciate those very elements of the past it was recently only too happy to destroy. At first, only the kitsch side of the nineteenth century received notice. But soon waxed flowers, long skirts and granny spectacles were followed by more serious indicators of a change in taste. Saleroom prices for Victorian art – once despised as coy and sentimental – increased. As the 'never had it so good' era faltered, the expensive cycle of razing and rebuilding was replaced by a more considered rehabilitation, and the Victorian Society began to accumulate powerful allies in its fight against destruction. By the 1980s the melange of architectural styles which had graced Victorian public buildings replaced the once ubiquitous concrete and plate-glass facades of commercial and government buildings. As the nineteenth century faded from popular memory, individuals began to pick and choose those elements of the recent past that best suited their needs in the changing landscape of the twentieth century.

But this revival of interest in the nineteenth century signalled a much more serious preoccupation with the past. During the last thirty years, Britain has ceased to be a world power. Her economy, although sustaining a modest increase in prosperity for most of the population, has fared less well than those of other nations, in particular the once despised states of the European Economic Community. Yet while the country plays only a tiny role in the decision-making of the superpowers, she maintains still a tacit intellectual and historic superiority in her dealings with the rest of the world. Not surprisingly, the nation's leaders, whose own personal fortunes depend so much on the perceived performance of the nation, look backward to those times when Britain appeared to lie less at the mercy of the economic and social forces beyond her control. In the public breast-beating during the last ten years about the state of the nation, Britain's days of glory in the nineteenth century are never far from politicians' lips, while the call for a return to the social values that supported that greatness has become a commonplace of political debate.

The precise nature of those values is something of a mystery, as is their much-vaunted potency as a cure for those social and economic ills that seem to afflict Britain more severely than her neighbours. Nevertheless, the message is clear: if Britain returns to the ethic of hard work, christian morality and financial prudence so popular three generations ago, the tidal wave of economic disaster may yet be turned. Here, at least, the rhetoric is Victorian, even if the values are not.

For these values are not what they seem. They represent Victorian society not as it was but as the conscientious social reformers and exporters of British culture to the empire would have liked it to be. These are the standards that figures as diverse as Lord Shaftesbury and Seebohm Rowntree tried to impose on the heterogenous millions who made up Victorian Britain. Their success lay not in the nineteenth century but in the twentieth, in the years between the death of Victoria and the outbreak of the Second World War, when the values they had hymned were accepted, and entered the fabric of existence for almost every class in Britain; ironically, in the light of our own preoccupations, at a time when Britain's power was already beginning to wane. We have thus simply inherited ideals of behaviour having no greater relation to the nineteenth century than they do to the present day.

This naïve association between success and Victorian values has allowed politicians to create in the past a political arcadia for the 1980s. This has masked the more substantial legacy of the nineteenth century to the present. For the greatest and most lasting achievement of the Victorians was their creation of institutions: the representative, democratic monarchy that we live under today; the civil service, whose edicts and requirements govern our everyday actions; the modern system of courts and legal administration, as well as a prison system barely reformed since the nineteenth century; the principle of an equal state education for all; and finally, the structure of devolved local government working to complement the activities of central administration. In fact, the whole superstructure of law and regulation that is conveniently termed the state was substantially the creation of the Victorian mind.

But this state was created from the struggles of the Victorian ruling classes to come to terms with the dramatic changes that half a century of industrialisation had forced on every aspect of their lives. We are now utilising these institutions within a society that has changed faster in the last hundred years than at any point in recorded history. The population of Britain today has perhaps a higher general level of education, more consumer power and less absolute need to work than ever before and many of the solutions proposed to the problems of government by the Victorians have an ever-decreasing relevance in the twentieth century.

For example, the form of democratic government eventually established in the nineteenth century guaranteed to each citizen (a definition expanded to include women and those between the ages of eighteen and twenty-one during the twentieth century) the right to vote for the member of Parliament of their choice on at least one day every seven, and later, five years. Yet neither individuals nor constituencies has any formal control over their MP, while the entire system is so crude in its operation that it is possible for a government to be elected that does not command a majority of the votes cast in an election. Perhaps the crudity of this system explains too the efforts of both Liberal and left-wing Labour activists to make the system more responsive to the electorate through the introduction of transferable voting or by exercising closer control over the actions of MPs in Parliament.

The legal system is another obvious example. In the nineteenth century, the state perfected a system of retributive imprisonment for law-breakers of almost every category. In this way the state made apparent to all its intention to protect society from the criminal and dangerous classes. But more than a century's research has still failed to prove that this form of social punishment has any appreciable deterrent effect. But, as in many other areas of government, tradition still triumphs over practicality, and the fact that neither politicians nor political theories have effected major reform to those Victorian institutions renders them no less obsolete in the late twentieth century.

In this book, we have tried to illuminate the ways in which these institutions and the attitudes they represent crystallised during those decades of the nineteenth century when every class was not only coming to terms with a new style of living, but also coming to terms with the idea that these living and working conditions might themselves continue to change.

Perhaps the biggest shift came in the mass migration from the land to the town which has only begun to slow in the last few decades. At the end of the eighteenth century, the majority of the population lived and worked on the land; by the end of the nineteenth, the majority lived in towns and worked in manufacturing or service industries. Ironically, Maxine Berg shows that it was precisely that thriving agricultural economy of the eighteenth century that provided both the capital and the labour necessary for the industrialisation that wrenched so many people from a way of life that was centuries old. With the profits from commerce and agriculture, the eighteenth-century entrepreneur was able to diversify into manufacturing and purchase the technology, often small-scale and domestic, that improved both the quality of his product and the speed at which it was made. In this way, water and steam were gradually harnessed to production, and complex machinery was finally introduced into the working lives of people all over Britain.

Although industrialisation did provoke a massive urbanisation of Britain's population, Penelope Corfield warns in her chapter against taking too simple a view of the process. She demonstrates that without the dynamic regional town life of the eighteenth century, the essential exchange between agriculture, capital and technical expertise would have been much retarded. For the towns provided the financial services to turn agricultural profits into industrial investments; they concentrated technical and commercial expertise; and, perhaps most important, they were centres of information and standards of consumption that influenced the whole country.

But change occurred on an individual level as well. Opportunities for better wages and more regular work in the manufactories and towns of the early nineteenth century created a new working class, divorced from the land and traditional social controls. In these unpromising conditions, urban workers created for themselves a culture diverging substantially from the accepted mores of Victorian middle-class society. By looking at the attitudes to education within this culture, Phillip Gardner demonstrates the strength and vitality it possessed and analyses the largely successful attempts of Victorian philanthropists to impose in its place their own ideas of acceptable social and family behaviour.

For the demands of industrialising Britain not only shaped new classes but reshaped old institutions, including the family. Traditionally, men and women had worked together on the land, as had children, and these practices were initially adopted within factories and urban workshops. But Catherine Hall's chapter suggests that as prosperity allowed the middle classes to dispense with the help of wives, mothers and children in the family business, so the world of work was separated from domestic life. This effectively confined women to the home and the care of children while transforming the world of work into an increasingly male preserve. And because the nineteenth-century middle class wielded disproportionate influence on the social customs of their day, these values were gradually imposed on all classes in Britain, whether they related to their own economic and social circumstances or not.

However, by the end of the nineteenth century the family that was divided by work could, and did, play together. James Walvin demonstrates how the industrial revolution eventually brought sufficient prosperity to the working classes to allow them to buy not only the necessities of everyday existence, but also that most precious of commodities, free time. Some forms of leisure were exclusively male, like football, or music-making in the popular brass bands, but the seaside holiday – whether a day trip by rail or a week beside the sea – united families of all classes in the enjoyment of fresh air, donkey rides and sea-bathing.

Society could not change so quickly without commensurate political change. But the pace of political change was slow and for much of the time kept firmly under the control of the political nation, those classes from whom were drawn parliamentarians, administrators and local politicians. For these classes, the first reaction to social change was terror. They saw there only the disorder that would topple the system of government that had suited them so well. Vic Gatrell looks at this perception in detail and explains how nineteenth-century parliaments began to preserve law and order at the expense of personal liberty. In the process they established the foundations of the bureaucratic state that still regulates our actions today. But the rights of the individual did expand in one particular area. In 1832 and 1867, the franchise was extended for the first time to the middle class and to certain 'respectable' sections of the working class. Michael Bentley investigates the reasons for this revolution in political thinking and shows that the advance of parliamentary democracy owed little to popular pressure or intellectual argument and almost everything to the political battles fought by Disraeli and Gladstone as they struggled to keep their respective parties in office.

The mentality of these classes, disproportionately important within the ever-growing population of Victorian Britain, is still something of a puzzle. Boyd Hilton and Peter Bowler offer two complementary insights into this character. Boyd Hilton demonstrates how the economic prosperity of the later Victorian period diminished uncertainty about the future. It prompted a change in religious belief that not only assured the middle class of a salvation commensurate with the status of their earthly life but also provided a philosophical justification for the amelioration of the society in which they lived, and perhaps led to the perception of social duty that lay behind the welfare-state thinking of the early nineteenth century.

Peter Bowler also focuses on the growing self-confidence of this influential grouping by probing their reaction to the discoveries of archaeologists and geologists which destroyed for ever the Biblical time-scale on which the Creation, and man's supreme place within that Creation, were based. Here the Victorians were able to survive this evidence of God's indifference by ignoring those facts that proved uncomfortable and inventing in their stead a distant past more suitable to their own perception of their place in the modern world.

For they were in no doubt that it was their society, and their values, that the wider world should see, admire and imitate. Roy Foster charts the ultimately unsuccessful attempt to amalgamate Ireland, by ideology and by violence, into that society. Quite separate from the rest of Britain in social and economic terms, Ireland itself was internally fragmented by religion and economic development in ways Westminster politicians could neither understand nor accommodate into their political plans. David Dabydeen looks at the same process from the point of view of Britain's overseas colonies. In both areas, assertive government provoked violence, and perhaps more dangerous, disaffection; the very reactions it had hoped to avoid by sharing the benefits of industrial civilisation.

Yet in the last years of Victoria's reign, Britain was still the most powerful nation in the world, even if the USA and Germany threatened as potential rivals. Perhaps the clue to this continued dominance lies in Michael Broers' chapter. Here he argues that Britain's victory over France in the revolutionary wars at the beginning of the century was so complete that her command of Europe was undisputed for the next hundred years. Furthermore, because the tiny nations of western Europe still controlled much of the rest of the globe through their empires the Victorians felt that they were the arbiters of both the politics and, more important, the commerce of the world. There was only one superpower in 1870, and it is perhaps because of this that we have preserved for so long the philosophical and institutional legacy of that time, Britain's last, and most glorious, golden age.

The Echo of the Tumbril

Michael Broers

The eighteenth century was a period of fierce competition among the major European powers for political and regional domination; it was an era when the greatness and viability of a state was judged in terms of war well-waged and diplomacy well-conducted. A series of European wars punctuate the history of the century, and the names posterity has given them denote a dynastic, rather than a national or ideological character: the War of Spanish Succession (1702–14); the War of Polish Succession (1733–38); and the War of Austrian Succession (1740–48), culminating in the Seven Years' War (1756–63). Most of the states involved in these conflicts were concerned with particular, localised objectives: Prussia and the Habsburg Empire fought two wars over the province of Silesia, on their mutual border in eastern Germany and, together with Russia, they disputed control of the collapsing kingdom of Poland. However, the major thread in eighteenth-century relations was the rivalry between Britain and France, which was of a much wider and more fundamental nature than that of the eastern monarchies. Britain and France were the greatest of the major powers and their conflict shaped the affairs of men and nations everywhere, from the moment in 1689 when William of Orange led Britain into a European coalition against Louis XIV, until Wellington finally defeated Napoleon at Waterloo in 1815. From across the Channel, these rivals confronted each other in what was nothing less than a second Hundred Years' War, but a war greater in scope than the knights of Crécy or Agincourt could ever have imagined, a war of vast, hitherto unknown proportions.

This is what set their conflict apart from the purely European ambitions of the other powers. Britain and France clashed directly with each other in all the major wars of the century, with the sole exception of the War of Polish Succession. However, they fought their battles less in Europe itself than in the non-European world. They alone of the European states were competing for colonies and trade, for although Spain, Portugal and the Netherlands still possessed vast colonial empires, only Britain and France were still able to think in terms of expansion, for the most part at each other's expense. Alone among the great powers, they had no territorial designs against each other; they did not crave each other's domestic provinces. Rather, their interest in the Seven Years' War, in particular, centred on the expansion of their colonies in North America and India, and on the control of the trans-Atlantic trade routes. Their armies did not fight each other at home but on the plains of India and in the forests of Canada and they, alone of the major powers, waged important naval campaigns. Thus, even in its geographical and military contexts, the Anglo-French contest was notably different from the rivalries of other states.

Anglo-French rivalry was different in quite another way as well, for it embraced not only a series of wars, but two of the most cataclysmic political events in the history of the western world, the French and American Revolutions. In this fact, just as much as in its long duration and far-flung nature, the magnitude of their conflict dominates the history of the eighteenth century. Theirs a clash of interests that came to embrace ideas as well as ambitions; it became a fight for

1.1. *The Black Watch at Bushy Run*, a painting by C. W. Geffreys

men's minds and for their very souls, if some of the protagonists are to be believed, as much as for land and power, colonies and wealth. Chronologically, however, these two political revolutions and the world wars they rekindled came at the end of the conflict and thus they represent its climax and finale, not its inception. The roots of Anglo-French rivalry are to be found in the social, economic and geographic forces which, by the last decades of the eighteenth century, had moulded Britain and France into imposing and almost equal rivals for world power. The duration of the conflict is testimony in itself to their parity of strength, but the sources of their strength were very different. It is important for their future development, in the course of the nineteenth century, to see how the final resolution of their conflict would accentuate, rather than diminish or obliterate, these differences.

Britain in the late eighteenth century was the economic hub of Europe. Regarded by economic and social thinkers on the continent as a model worthy of imitation, she had a small but rapidly growing population, which had risen from about seven and a half million around 1760 to nearly nine and half million by 1780, and to twelve and a quarter million by 1811.[1] Britain possessed a powerful industrial base which, if limited by modern standards, was then unique in Europe in three crucial ways. Although still a predominantly agricultural country, Britain's industrial sector was far larger than any other European state's; more than that, it was technologically more advanced than its rivals and, finally, it was supported by the highly advanced financial and commercial institutions of the City of London, then as now the money-market of Europe, which provided British commerce and industry with credit facilities absent on the continent. Her system of government was equally unique among the great powers, in the extensive authority which was vested in Parliament. Where representative bodies existed on the continent, their authority extended only to particular provinces and never over a whole state. None of them, not even a body as powerful as the *parlement* of Paris, could share in the sovereignty of a whole nation, or claim to represent the interests and opinions of the population as a whole. The elective nature of the British Parliament was less singular as regards its social composition, which was as elitist as many diets and estates on the continent, as in the frequency of its elections, which were definitely fixed as every seven years by an Act of 1716. Above all, by the 1770s Britain had acquired a vast colonial empire in India and North America, largely at the expense of France, and had emerged as the greatest maritime power in the world.

France, by contrast, was a landbound Leviathan that dominated her continental neighbours by the sheer size of her territories, which were over twice the size of Britain, and by her population which numbered close to twenty-five million by the late eighteenth century. From this basis, France fielded the great land armies which were her reply to the 'wooden walls' of the British navy, and to which the small German and Italian states had no effective answer. All of this earned France the contemporary label of 'the China of Europe'. In contrast to the parliamentary system in Britain, France was ruled by a seemingly absolute monarch from the 'Imperial city' at Versailles, without elected institutions, but with a pomp and circumstance commensurate with her status as the greatest land power in Europe. The French economy was overwhelmingly rural and the vast majority of the people were peasants engaged in primitive subsistence farming, as was the norm all over Europe in this period. Nonetheless, France still boasted the only commercial sector in Europe remotely capable of rivalling British supremacy since the decline of the Dutch in the late seventeenth century. Nantes, Bordeaux and Cherbourg, the great Atlantic ports, fought for the world market with Bristol and Liverpool, while Marseilles, her Mediterranean outlet, probably took a larger share of southern trade than did Britain. As a great power, with a great power's ambitions, France looked to the development of her overseas trade and her own empire, which entailed continually accepting the challenge posed by Britain, even after the loss of Canada and much of India by 1763.

Thus, in the last quarter of the eighteenth century, as the conflict entered its final stages, France stood poised for revenge, awaiting a chance to recover her losses, with her seemingly bottomless human resources and great land armies ready, once again, to assail British naval and industrial might.

That chance came in 1775, when dissent over taxation in Britain's thirteen American colonies erupted into full-scale war, the American Revolution. The Americans began their struggle in an attempt to reassert their traditional rights as Englishmen against what they felt to be an increasingly corrupt and despotic imperial government, but when the crisis evolved into a war for outright independence, the ex-colonists were quick to accept help from France, an unashamedly absolutist state. Set in a global context, it is no coincidence that the court of Versailles was the first state to recognise the new American Republic, and France intervened forcefully and decisively on the side of the colonists, an act which was instrumental in dislodging the British from the most valuable part of their empire. The importance of French participation in the American Revolution is epitomised by the crucial part played by the French fleet in the Yorktown campaign of 1781, which ended the war. It was an essential contribution to the American

1.2. The surrender of
Lord Cornwallis during
the American War of
Independence

cause at a time when the new state had no effective navy of its own.

However, in terms of the Anglo-French rivalry, the American victory solved almost nothing. Britain was not dislodged from the rest of her empire while, as the 'workshop of the world', she continued to dominate the economic life of the newly created United States of America, even if her political role had ceased. The French did not regain their colonies, and emerged from the war with a huge national debt which would bankrupt the monarchy by the late 1780s and contribute to its downfall. The chance to break the deadlock had been missed by both sides, and the most important single result of the American Revolution was to create a new nation which would become the most powerful state in history. It is true that the protest of the colonists had disturbed the consciences of many within the British political nation and impressed on men as different as the radical Thomas Paine and the arch-conservative Edmund Burke, the need to value and preserve the essence of the British political system, but this was not the central issue of the years to come. However inspiring and thought-provoking the spectacle of American rebellion was for contemporaries, it was enacted thousands of miles away, on the fringes of an empty and still unknown hemisphere. For most

Europeans it was less an example to be imitated than the final confirmation that the New World could, and would, be dominated by European culture and by people of European descent, now strong enough to colonise the New World without direct political and military support from Europe. It did little, then, to resolve the wider conflict between Britain and France, but the next, most dramatic and unforeseen event in their relationship would, indeed, prove decisive, and that was the outbreak of revolution in France itself.

In direct contrast to events in America, the French Revolution took place at the heart of European civilisation; it changed and galvanised the most powerful and populous state in Europe, and it all occurred only a few miles off the British coast. For British observers, the French Revolution was important not only in its ideological aspects, but also because of its unpredictable repercussions for Anglo-French rivalry. It would soon become clear that the revolution's ideological aspects could not long be ignored or separated from other issues; it turned a war on one front, that of conventional great power rivalry, into a war on two, as it became essential to combat the new ideas of the old rival, as well as her traditional ambitions.

The French Revolution was, above all else, an experiment in representative and constitutional government, and one which took place at a stunning pace. The political and administrative institutions of France went through several fundamental transformations within a remarkably short space of time. By the summer of 1789, the concept of absolute monarchy was breached in practice, when Louis XVI called a nationally elected body, the Estates General, to help him frame tax reforms. This body had not met since 1614, and it is a clear sign of the crown's financial desperation that it took such a step. The Estates General soon converted itself into a National Assembly and was able to force a constitution and an elected legislature on the king by 1791. The outbreak of war in 1792, and Louis XVI's own reluctance to adhere to the constitution, led to even more radical changes. By 1793, the king had been deposed and beheaded, and a republic proclaimed, ruled by a new National Convention, elected by universal manhood suffrage.

This swift transformation was partly due to the intrinsic weaknesses of the old order in France, but its speed and coherence depended above all on the ideological clarity of the revolutionaries, at least in the initial stages of reform, who found in the political thought of the eighteenth century a clear plan for the restructuring of civil society. Although still untested and abstract, the theories of the writers of the Enlightenment provided the reformers of 1789 with a clear conceptual basis for the new political culture they set out to create. The old provinces, whose names are still household words in England as well

1.3 The execution of
Louis XVII

as France, were abolished. Normandy, Brittany, Burgundy and
Provence disappeared, to be replaced by smaller units, the departments.
The Church, too, was reformed, stripped of its legal privileges and
much of its property. Predictably, these reforms were very unpopular
with large segments of French society and they produced serious
rebellions in many parts of France. Nonetheless, the whole process set
an example of how new patterns of political behaviour could emerge
within the framework of a traditional European society.

It was a powerful invitation to imitation by others, and one which
the British ruling classes found increasingly alarming and distasteful.
As early as 1790, Edmund Burke, who had championed the American
cause a decade earlier, pointed to the changed social complexion of
the new rulers of France

the general composition was of obscure provincial advocates . . .
county attorneys . . . the fomentors and conductors of the petty war
of village vexations.[2]

The French revolutionaries were, that is, drawn from elements in
society who were not, in the eyes of British patricians, fit to rule.

It was their foreign policy, however, that worried more practical
politicians, especially the prime minister of the period, William Pitt the

Younger. In 1792, the revolutionaries declared, as they put it, 'war on the chateau and peace on the cottage', and openly expressed their willingness to help other peoples to 'liberate themselves'. That is, they were the originators of that most twentieth-century of pastimes, exporting revolution. Pitt preferred to describe their new mixture of ideology and foreign policy as

> calculated everywhere to sow the seeds of rebellion and civil contention, and to spread war from one end of Europe to the other, from one end of the globe to another.[3]

War did, indeed, come; Britain and France had rejoined the old struggle by January 1793. The ideological threat, a new element in the conflict, had been forged into a real threat because for all the turmoil within France, she was still a great power, possessed of the resources of a great power, which the revolutionaries were able to marshal far more ably than the old monarchy ever had. By 1793, through a staggering feat of organisation and ruthlessness, 350,000 men had been put into the field. Lord Castlereagh, who later played a leading role in the British war effort and who was the architect of France's final defeat, noted in that year:

> we contend with an opponent whose strength we have no means of measuring. It is the first time that all the population and all the wealth of a great kingdom has been concentrated in the field.

Even after nearly two centuries, his dread fear of the course of events can be readily sensed, as he concluded, 'what may be the result is beyond my perception'.[4]

Castlereagh was a man of exceptional intelligence, and it was unlikely that what followed could have been predicted. France was plunged into her own bitter civil war, which produced a further gallery of different regimes. The intensity of this civil war within the Revolution itself is reflected in the extremes represented by the succession of governments between 1793 and 1799. The 'Jacobin dictatorship' of Robespierre and the Committee of Public Safety has come to symbolise the Revolution at its most radical; this was the period of the Terror and the height of popular involvement in politics, at least in urban centres. Although seriously exaggerated by the partisan histories of both Left and Right,[5] the Terror period undoubtedly saw more popular participation in politics than the 'bourgeois republic' known as the Directory, which succeeded it. These moderate republicans took power in a purge as violent and divisive as any of those perpetrated under the Terror. The violence with which

1.4. *The Coronation of Napoleon 1804*, by David

1.5. The 'wooden walls' of the Royal Navy

they ousted Robespierre created a gulf between moderate and radical republicans which was never fully healed, while the new regime was equally unsuccessful in appeasing French royalists. Thus isolated and assailed from two political extremes, the Directory gave way, almost unwittingly, to the military dictatorship of Napoleon Bonaparte. Bonaparte was brought to power in an effort to preserve the republic from self-destruction from within. He was able to restrain the republican factions and keep the royalist threat at bay, and was able to declare himself emperor in 1804, ruling as such until 1814.

What is remarkably consistent in all this is that, in foreign policy, France continued to act, and to fight, as the aggressive great power she still was, regardless of who ruled her. This fact was not lost on the author of *Address to the People of the United Kingdom of Great Britain and Ireland on the threat of Invasion*, written in 1803, who told his readers that Napolean was 'as prodigal of human blood as Robespierre, Marat and Danton',[6] the leaders of the most radical phase of the Revolution. That is, the deep-rooted rivalry between Britain and France went its bloody way unhindered, if not untouched, by questions of ideology. The military pattern too, remained the same, but on a scale spectacular even by its past standards. The French armies swept across Europe between 1792 and 1812, while the British navy swept the seas. By 1803, while England stood once more behind her wooden walls, Napoleon's Grand Army of 500,000 men stood powerless at its base in Boulogne. When they turned eastwards, however, French arms on land destroyed one British-financed coalition of continental allies after another. In 1804 Nelson's resounding naval victory at Trafalgar was soon outshone by the 'sun of Austerlitz', where Napoleon crushed the combined armies of Russia and Austria. He did the same to Prussia at Jena and Austerdat in 1806, and again to Austria at Wagram in 1809. Although checked in Spain in 1810–11, by 1812 Napoleon had redrawn the map of Europe to an unprecedented extent but he, in his turn, had watched powerless as Britain confiscated the remains of France's colonies almost at will, and had seen his grandiose plan of economic warfare, the Continental Blockade, disintegrate under the impact of British industrial might. In many important respects, little had changed; the two Titans had fought each other to a standstill. Perhaps the conflict can be given a more human scale when it is remembered that Pitt died in 1807, with no end in sight, and a sense of human perspective is gained in the knowledge that he was the son of the Earl of Chatham, 'the Great Commoner', William Pitt the Elder, who had been the architect of Britain's victory over France a generation before, in 1763.

When the deadlock was finally broken, it came with Napoleon's crushing defeat by the Russian winter and not, significantly, through a direct confrontation with his country's archrival. As the depleted French armies were pushed back to their own borders between 1812 and 1814, Britain stood ready, and almost unscathed, to finish off forever the challenge of French ambition. If the Russian snows had turned the tide, it was Britain who would ride it to victory, with her industry and empire secure and intact, her homeland untouched by invasion or by direct contact with the work of the Revolution. It is significant that in 1814 Britain's post-war position was so strong that Castlereagh exercised the single most powerful influence at the Congress of Vienna, which was to reshape Europe following the collapse of the Napoleonic empire. Castlereagh's role was a more indirect one than that of Metternich, the Austrian foreign minister, but little could be achieved against his decided opposition, and it was due chiefly to him that France was given a constitutional government in 1814.

But preserving Britain from revolution and invasion had not been easy. Twenty years of dogged determination and effort had left its own deep impression on the life of the nation. There is no real doubt that the ideology of the French Revolution was rejected by all but a minority in Britain. This minority was a colourful and articulate one, it is true, and its glamorous proponents – the English Jacobins, the Friends of Liberty, the United Englishmen, Irishmen and Scotsmen – have attracted the attention of colourful and articulate historians. Marianne Elliott on the United Irishmen and Roger Wells on the British radicals of the 1790s, are the most recent and exciting exponents of a field of interest pioneered by Edward Thompson in his classic work, *The Making of the English Working Class*.[7] However, by concentrating so heavily on the radical minority, it is arguable that too little attention has been paid to the conservative majority of Britons. Nonetheless, their conspiracies and pamphlets brought out the repressive instincts of Lord Eldon, the hard-pressed Home Secretary of the day. Eldon was far from an isolated figure in his fear of the 'Jacobinal tide', for as early as 1792, 'Loyalist Associations' had been formed by the local propertied elites all over the country, devoted not just to the defence of the realm but also, as the parent Association in London declared, 'to defend persons and property from French principles'.[8] Two could play at ideological warfare, and the fact is that the counter-revolutionaries were far better at it than their pro-French opponents. Perhaps the saddest case among these 'Friends of Liberty' was Tom Paine, author of the 'radical bible' of the times, *The Rights of Man*. Driven from England in 1792, charged with treason, he fled to France, where the National Convention elected him 'deputy for the constituency of mankind'. Soon after the outbreak of war in 1793,

Paine found himself behind French bars, as a direct result of the xenophobia that swept the country. His case is a poignant testimony to the enduring power of the rivalry between these two states.

It is interesting that two quite different strands of propaganda emerged in the ideological battle for the mind and soul of the nation. The first was directed at the propertied classes, and dwelt on the liberal and democratic aspects of the Revolution – on the threat to property and to the traditional character of British politics; for the weekly journal *The Anti-Jacobin* the enemy was 'Jacobinism in all its shapes, and in all its degrees, political and moral, public and private, whether as it openly threatens the subversion of states, or gradually saps the foundations of domestic happiness.'[9] Perhaps the real genius of this propaganda, however, was its subtlety, a discerning approach which kept the ruling classes together, because it made room for those who had often favoured reforms before the war, even, ultimately, for Charles James Fox, the bumptious leader of the Opposition, who had stubbornly championed the Revolution, but was finally drawn into the war effort by 1806. Fox had always been in a minority and, indeed, often all but alone. Far more significant for upper-class unity were the arguments of Edmund Burke, who extolled the traditional liberty of British parliamentary government, and who was able to portray the struggle against the Revolution as one to preserve liberty, rather than defeat it. Indeed, the strength of these institutions and liberties often checked the government's own security measures. Although, for example, Parliament voted for the suspension of *Habeus Corpus* in 1793, the following year saw a jury drawn from the propertied classes acquit three prominent radicals – John Thelwall, Thomas Hardy and Horne Took – of charges of treason.[10] In the end, the success of Burke's approach emphasises how wedded to their indigenous ways the British elite was, a bond which the struggle with France served to reinforce.

Popular propaganda was quite different; no distinction was drawn between past conflicts and the new one, that is to say, the ideological element was markedly underplayed for the masses or, at least, presented in a very different manner from the columns of *The Anti-Jacobin*. Popular propaganda was all the more effective for this different emphasis and drew with great skill on the traditional, ingrained fears of French tyranny, echoing folk-memories of the 'Norman Yoke', as reflected in the titles of such popular tracts as *John Bull turned into a galley slave*. Indeed, the ability to exploit the myth of the 'Norman Yoke' became even easier after Napoleon seized power. 'The Corsican Tyrant' was readily equated with Louis XIV and William the Conqueror, while he was also portrayed comically, most enduringly as Gillray's 'Little Boney', who first appeared in 1803 and

1.6. *Little Boney* by Gillray

has remained a stock figure in British satire and humour ever since. All of this was sharpened by the very real threat of invasion, which united almost everyone and produced propaganda based on a blend of fear and contemptuous humour remarkably akin to that engendered by similar circumstances in 1939–45.

By the first years of the new century the conflict with France, and the fear of all things French, was too deeply impressed on people's thinking for the minority of English Jacobins to make much headway. They tried, of course, and the role of political agitators in events like the great naval mutinies of 1797 may well have been underrated by historians until quite recently. It had long been assumed that the mutinies in the Channel and North Sea fleets were merely protests against poor pay and serving conditions, but it has recently been shown that they had a deeply political nature. The sailors were strongly influenced by radical politics and their demands went far beyond their immediate concerns, embracing electoral reform and demands for peace with France.[11] All this notwithstanding, when the moment of decision came the sailors did not go over to the French. Although the authorities greatly feared that French invasion would produce a social revolution, had this happened it would have been a unique event in the history of the period. Despite their declared objectives, it was the French armies, and not those of the old order, which met popular resistance in Italy, the Rhineland and, most spectacularly, in Spain, where the cry 'Church and King' came to symbolise a rabid, fanatical resistance to the Revolution.

This, of course, is pure speculation in a British context. The reality was that the nation was preserved from such searching tests. No kings were killed, no ancient institutions swept away, no charges of collaboration coloured the mainstream of British politics, even if they tinted its fringes. In all of this, Britain was unique in Europe. Every state the French occupied for any length of time adopted the political and legal institutions developed by the Revolution. The *Code Napoléon*, which embodied the essence of the legal reforms of the Revolution, became the basis for the judicial systems of all the major states of western Europe in the nineteenth century. In similar fashion the French administrative structure, with its system of centrally appointed and controlled local officials, became the norm in the states of today's European community. These were currents which never touched Britain, in common with other states on the fringes of Europe such as Russia and Spain, and from which her victory itself set her even further apart.

The final defeat of France was of more than purely European importance because it left Britain unchallenged in the wider world; she entered the nineteenth century without any serious naval, colonial or economic rivals. She turned this new freedom into a 'splendid isolation', a cutting adrift from Europe, which would last well into the new century and allow her unique culture and society to take its own path in an era of rapid and fundamental change. The clash of Titans was over; the *pax Britannica* had begun.

Further reading

T.C.W. Blanning, *The Origins of the French Revolutionary Wars* (Oxford, 1986); I.R. Christie, *Crisis of Empire: Great Britain and the American Colonies* (New York, 1966); I.R. Christie, *Wars and Revolutions, 1760–1815*, vol. 7 of the Arnold 'New History of England' (London, 1982); J. Ehrman, *The Younger Pitt*, vol. 2 (London, 1983); C. Emsley, *British Society and the French Wars, 1793–1815* (London, 1979); D. McKay and H.M. Scott, *The Rise of the Great Powers, 1648–1815* (London, 1983); E.S. Morgan, *The Birth of the Republic, 1763–1789* (Chicago and London, 1977); D. Sutherland, *Revolution and Counter-Revolution in France, 1789–1815* (London, 1986); R. Wells, *Insurrection, the British Experience, 1795–1803* (Gloucester, 1983).

CHAPTER TWO

A Question of Machinery

Maxine Berg

I Industrial Revolution or slow growth?

We look back to the Industrial Revolution as the great turning point in our history – as the beginning and indeed cause of our modern society. Eric Hobsbawm described it as 'the most fundamental transformation of human life in the history of the world recorded in written documents. For a brief period it coincided with the history of a single country, Great Britain'.[1] The words themselves convey images of new technology and industry, the steam engine and the cotton mill. Historians in recent times endorsed these images in their analyses of economic growth, capital investment and the cataclysmic processes of technological change. Politicians still take comfort in a history of days of greatness when innovation, flexible labour markets and dynamic entrepreneurs with little state interference ensured economic success. This Industrial Revolution was a Prometheus, and it was not unlike the perceptions of those in the 1830s and 1840s who saw themselves as living through an *Age of Machinery*. Thomas Carlyle spoke of 'The huge demon of Mechanisation ... changing his shape like a very Proteus ... and infallibly at every change of shape, oversetting whole multitudes of workmen.' Sarcastically encapsulating the attitudes of many of his contemporaries, he pronounced on the new locomotives, 'These are our poems'. James Nasmyth, the celebrated engineer, expressed some ambiguous feelings on his visit to the Black Country in 1830. 'Amidst these flaring, smoky, clanging works I beheld the remains of what had once been happy farmhouses, now ruined and deserted.' The workmen in the blast furnaces 'seemed to be running about amidst the flames as in a pandemonium'.[2]

But now historians have turned to a much more gradualist interpretation of the Industrial Revolution, a phenomenon stretching

2.1. *Science Making Giant Strides*, by George Cruickshank

back to the early days of the eighteenth century and continuing at least until the mid nineteenth century. Population was growing and agriculture improving from the earliest years of the eighteenth century; indeed there is substantial evidence that major increases in yields and labour productivity in agriculture were achieved by the yeomen farmers of seventeeth-century England.[3] Working people were increasingly occupied in non-agricultural occupations – in the service sector and industrial crafts – from the late seventeenth century, and to a much greater extent than we once thought. Towns were growing at a rate unique in Europe. There was thus a growth in numbers, food, industries and towns from early in the eighteenth century.

But the Industrial Revolution, as it has always been, remains a terrain for debate and interpretation among historians. Though most now endorse a more evolutionary path of change, there is still considerable conflict of opinion over the extent of change and its implications. Some historians back their opinions by greater use of quantitative evidence and the revision and technical manipulation of estimates of growth and structural change.[4] But their opinions remain no better than the evidence and the methods they use.

The change in our interpretation of the Industrial Revolution also follows on shifts in our own current economic and political climate. Attempts to dispense with the notion of revolution, to find continuities with the earlier craft economies, to trace back the roots of slow growth to the former magic years of the eighteenth and early nineteenth centuries are histories written from our own despondent times. Once we looked back to the Industrial Revolution for our days of glory; here was a clear demonstration of a time of rapid economic growth, of the achievements of the factory system and large-scale technologies. Today we approach the Industrial Revolution with a great deal more hesitation, indeed doubt. Now we are questioning the sacred cows of the post-war boom – heavy capital investment, large-scale industry, new technology and structural change. Their ultimate failings and current social dislocation have been placed beside processes of decentralisation, new small-scale information technology and the revival of alternative small-scale and co-operative units. Now the history of past glories is not enough – we want answers to new, more relevant questions. We want to know just how rapid economic growth in the Industrial Revolution really was and the extent to which this growth was experienced across all industries and regions. Our current de-industrialisation of the North of England had its mirror image in the eighteenth century in a de-industrialisation of the South. But our histories tell us little of what happened to these people. Was there a great social divide then as now between the employed and the unemployed? We need to discover if the concept of employment meant the same in the past, and if day-to-day work was structured as it is now. And one of our major current concerns is the introduction of new technologies. Just how did the great inventions affect jobs and how did people react to them? Now we want to look at the failures as well as the success stories of industrialisation; at the controversies and conflicts underpinning change, not just the results in the final indices of economic growth.

II   Genesis of industrialisation

The really big shift we identify with the Industrial Revolution is the rise of the factory system. But how pervasive was it and how efficient compared to other industrial structures? The factory spread first in the cotton industry, but it is important to realise that this was a tiny industry in the eighteenth century, accounting for only 2.6 per cent of value added in British industry, while the woollen industry dominated with 30.6 per cent. Indeed, cotton did not become the most important of the textile industries until the 1820s.[5]

With this picture of an Industrial Revolution in greater continuity with its past than we previously thought, let us look back to the genesis of industrialisation. Who were the recruits to industry? Who organised and financed the new ventures, and where did they go? What differences did the new factories and machines make to the methods and organisation of production?

If we look to the engine room of most eighteenth-century industrial growth, the crucial input was not machines or capital, but labour, and enormous quantities of it. Most manufacture was labour-intensive – machines and factories before the nineteenth century were generally rudimentary. But labour was in abundant supply; population grew from 4.93 million in 1681 to 7.74 million in 1791. By 1831 England had 13.28 million inhabitants and Scotland 2.37 million: the rate of growth of their population had far outstripped that of all other Western European countries.[6] Not only were there more people, but there were fewer opportunities of eking out a living on the land. Agrarian change – the enclosure of areas of land long held in common and the major shift in many areas during the eighteenth century from the cultivation and rotation of various corn crops to permanent pasture for livestock production – destroyed the subsistence economies of the landless cottagers. Those in the Feldon of South Warwickshire had used the common land, sometimes as squatters and sometimes to combine some village craft with this small but significant stake in the land. Though they lived on the land they were occupied not only in agricultural, but in a whole range of retailing and industrial activities.

Enclosure drove them into a narrow range of lesser crafts – carpentry, tailoring and shoemaking – and rural poverty. Thomas Bewick commented that by enclosure of the commons, 'the poor man was rooted out, and the various mechanics of the village deprived of all benefit of it'. And Arthur Young endorsed the truth of the poor man's grievance. 'Parliament may be tender of property; all I know is, I had a cow, and an Act of Parliament has taken it from me.' Thus the population of the countryside grew – creating in some regions the poor, dispossessed and willing workforce for cheap putting-out industries, mines and rural factories; in others an entrenched largely unemployed agricultural labour force, immobilised by the rules of the Old Poor Law that parish relief would be paid only to those resident in the parish where they were born or who had obtained a settlement qualification.[7]

Much of Britain's industrialisation was played out in rural locations, or alternatively in small manufacturing towns whose population soon took off. It was not the metropolis, county towns or large pre-industrial urban centres that attracted new industry, but new manufacturing towns integrated into rural industrial regions. Birmingham, Manchester, Sheffield, Leeds and Liverpool were the results of the 'industrialisation from below'. Birmingham grew from 8000 in 1700 to 74,000 in 1800. Already in 1755, a visitor found Birmingham,

> another *London* in miniature . . . the lower part is filled with the workshops and warehouses of the manufacturers . . . the upper part . . . contains a number of new, regular streets, and a handsome square all well built and well-inhabited.[8]

The population of its surrounding industrial villages was anonymous and mobile. At the beginning of the eighteenth century, to be sure, most people still lived in the countryside but they were not merely agricultural labourers; they practised all kinds of domestic industry and petty retailing, they swelled the burgeoning mining and building workforces and they went into the factories which until the nineteenth century were mainly located in the countryside close to sources of water power. Britain's Industrial Revolution grew out of a pre-existing rural industrial heritage.

But the new industries also drew, in ways we have now lost sight of, on women's and children's labour. Early industrial expansion was dominated by textiles, and women and children made up by far the greatest part of the textile labour force. The point was made by Adam Smith when he wrote in *The Wealth of Nations* that the spinners were far more important to the cloth industry than any other group of

2.2. The spinning jenny

workers and 'our spinners are poor people, women especially, scattered about in different parts of the country without support or protection.' Estimates show that before mechanisation women and children accounted for 75 per cent of the workforce in the woollen industry. The first wave of mechanisation hit both men and women, but the dislocation to the female workforce with the new spinning techniques was far greater. The spinning jenny reduced the number of women employed per cloth to 18 per cent of its former total by the simple process of multiplying the number of spindles turned by a single wheel from one to anywhere from 16 to 40 initially, and within two years up to 120. But some women found work in the new textile factories as spinners, as spinners on the other new spinning machine, the water frame, or as carders, hand- and powerloom weavers and calico printers. The image of male virility conveyed by hammer and anvil in the metal trades is quite misplaced, for in the eighteenth century the central position was held by those women nailmakers discovered by William Hutton on the road to Birmingham in 1741, 'stript of their upper garment not overcharged with their lower, wielding the hammer with all the grace of their sex'. Then there were the skilled buttonworkers, small hardware and ornamental ware manufacturers such as the radical George Jacob Holyoake's mother, who ran a horn-button workshop behind her house while she brought up her children and ran her home.[9]

George Jacob Holyoake himself started working at home at the age of 7 or 8 soldering the handles on lanterns. At the age of 9 he was taken on at the foundry where his father was a foreman. His experience was the common one of children whose labour was integral to handicraft industry as well as factory production. Dean Tucker observed in 1758:

> In many provinces of the Kingdom, particularly Staffordshire, Lancashire, and certain districts of Yorkshire, with the Towns of Manchester, Norwich and some others, labour . . . is very properly proportioned . . . so that no Time shall be wasted in passing the goods to be manufactured from Hand to Hand, and that no unnecessary Strength should be employed . . . at Birmingham. viz. When a Man stamps on a metal Button by means of an Engine, a Child stands by him to replace the button in readiness to receive the Stamp, and to remove it when received, and then to place another. By these Means the Operator can stamp at least double the Number, when he could otherwise have done, had he been obliged to have stopped each Time to have shifted the Buttons: And as his Gettings may be from 14d to 18d and the Child's from a Penny to 2d per day for doing the same Quantity of Work, which must have require double the Sum, had the Man alone been employed; this single Circumstance saved alone 80, or even 100 per cent at the same Time that it trains up Children to an Habit of Industry, almost as soon as they can speak.

This assumption of the necessity of widespread child labour to the efficiency of industrial production is alien to our current ideas about work. While today one of our most pressing social problems is youth unemployment, pre-industrial and early industrial manufacture drafted in the labour of young teenagers and small children at the earliest opportunity. Crompton was the inventor of the spinning mule, which was a clever combination of parts from the water frame and the spinning jenny. He was a man in no great want, yet he set his infant son, soon after he could walk, to work cleaning cotton wool by treading on it in strong soapy water. The lot of poorer children was much worse. William Hutton was apprenticed to the Derby silk mill when he was still too short to reach the engines, and to reach them he had a set of pattens locked to his feet. In Northamptonshire children were sent out to lace schools at the age of 5 to start out on a 5–8-hour day and soon going on to a regular 12–14 hours. Those who stayed at home to work were rarely better off.[10] Ben Brierly remembered his initiation to labour:

> And now came the time that I had to be put to work. I had played at pulling the 'idle bant' when the cloggers apprentices were cross

cutting timber for my soles; I had played at turning a handle in the Bower Lane rope work . . . but now I must work . . . I was put to the bobbin wheel. How I hated being chained to the stool.

The Scottish handloom weaver's household was no comfort to his child employees. A government inspector reported in 1833:

The occupation of draw-boys and girls to harness loom weavers in their own shops is by far the lowest and least sought after of any connected with the cotton trade . . . they work as long as the weavers, that is, as long as they can see; standing on the same spot, barefooted, on an earthen cold damp floor in a close damp cellar, for thirteen or fourteen hours a day. They earn two shillings per week.[11]

The most lucrative source of child labour, however, was that of adolescents, especially young girls, employed then, as young women are now in the microelectronics sectors, for their nimble fingers, docility and attention to monotonous repetitive labour. Girls in calico-

2.3. A calico-printing workshop

printing workshops were employed to enormous profit by Robert Peel
to paint designs on the cloth by hand or to outline designs on printing
blocks by hammering in pins, as many as 10,000 to a single block.
The labour of several of them at these primitive methods was cheaper
than that of a single skilled calico-printer using more advanced block
and copper-plate printing.[12]

If labour came from the land, capital and enterprise also had
agrarian roots. Now, when international financial institutions and
massive capital provide the framework for industrial finance, it is hard
to imagine the relatively small sums generally required in the
eighteenth century to start out, and the unconventional sources of this
capital. Samuel Bamford described the road to riches taken by some
alongside the enduring poverty of those like himself. He remembered a
small bleacher called Hulme who had works at Belmont near Bolton.
He first came round with a one-horse cart collecting calicoes, and as
he was a steady and industrious man he got on fast and his
employment increased. He next appeared with a cart drawn by two
stout horses; soon after he had a waggon and in a short time as many
waggons as his business required with men to drive them and collect
pieces for him.[13]

Land, even the smallholding, was an important source of capital in
textile, iron and metal trades since it could be mortgaged to provide
starting capital. But the rural community itself was just as important.
Our image of the entrepreneur as an individual financing his enterprise
on abstinence and hard work is little more than Victorian myth. In
reality one of the greatest sources of capital was kin and neighbourhood networks. Lending cash to neighbours was a tradition of early
modern England. In the early phases of industrialisation some
communities were still close knit enough to carry such traditions over
into industrial finance. The small clothiers of the West Riding of
Yorkshire mortgaged their land, borrowed from kin and neighbours
and also drew on the banks – community connections created credit-
worthiness.[14] But alongside the common run of small-scale enterprise,
there was a significant number of industrial giants. Very few of these
built their success from rags to riches, but rather on family wealth
amassed in earlier generations in foreign trade and in the mercantile
networks of those who organised the dispersed rural industries.
Mathew Boulton, the 'iron chieftan' employed 500 in his hardware
and toy works by the 1770s, building on substantial capital left by his
father, who had started in the trade, and on his wife's sizeable dowry.

Opportunities for such enterprise and employment for labour were
not of course uniform over the country. The expanding industrial
regions of the West Midlands and the North had their backdrop in the
grim litany of industrial decline of the country's major textile centres

of the seventeenth and eighteenth centuries. Berkshire, Dorset, Hampshire, Wiltshire, Norfolk, Suffolk and Essex all dropped an average of 11 places in the county league table of wealth between 1693 and 1843. The present concentration of wealth in the south of England is a recent phenomenon. Throughout the later eighteenth and nineteenth centuries the reverse held true – a poorly paid de-industrialised South and the high-wage, industrial North.

Land and rural society provided the roots and incubator of early industrialisation, but there were, nevertheless, striking changes in the organisation of industrial production and its technology that really defined the novelty of the times. The factory system, as pointed out already, spread initially in a very small eighteenth-century industry – cotton manufacture. But why did it arise in the first place?

The classic advantages of the factory system were its improvement in labour discipline, and its success in controlling the quality of the product and reducing the embezzlement of raw materials. Contrary to popular assumption, advantages did *not* lie in necessary improvements in technical efficiency. The clothiers of Minchinhampton in 1780 complained about their domestic spinners, 'our poor spoil their yarn by dirtiness, bad spinning, damping and frequently putting several workers' yarns together'. Woollen Acts dictated the time allocated for artisans to complete and return their work, but prosecutions were numerous. Domestic workers also frequently embezzled for their own use raw materials provided by a factor or merchant for the production of finished goods. The opportunities for such theft allowed by a system where the employer was absent from and did not supervise the production process were ample. In 1768 Abigail Russell of Colchester 'put out as much of her master's yarne as did make her husband a pair of stockings, and last week as much as knitt a pair of child's stockings and stockt a paire for herselfe'. In 1764 Lydia Longbottom of Bingley was 'publicly whipt thro' the market at Wakefield, for working false and short yarn . . . the town bailiff carrying a reel before her'.[15]

Factories also had the added advantage, regarded as very important in the eighteenth century, of protecting inventions from the prying eyes of spies and foreign agents, and of providing a fortress against potential crowds of machine-breakers. Businesses in Birmingham were conducted in an atmosphere of secrecy; with cautions against 'showing workshops to strangers' and patterns, prices and terms of credit all kept secret. When a French agent and engineer, Gabriel Jars, tried to spy on sulphuric acid production at a secure plant near Wandsworth, London, he found that further precautions had been taken: 'I only met girls from Wales there of whom only a very small number knew even a few words of English. This precaution is doubtless taken so that they cannot divulge anything that happens in the laboratory.' James

Hargreaves' spinning jenny and Richard Arkwright's water frame were for a time kept within factory 'safe boxes' where only trusted workmen were admitted and with no windows on the bottom floor.

The factory may have helped to reduce day-by-day problems of labour discipline and to protect patents for a time. But the domestic system also contained its own internal disciplines and advantages. One of these disciplines was the widespread indebtedness of workers to masters and merchants. Peter Stubs, the Warringon fileworker, wrote of a workman tied by debt to another firm, but so anxious to work for Stubs that he was willing to transfer to him the rights to the labour of his sons who were then apprenticed to their father.[16] The domestic system was also a very good cushion for economic fluctuations. Dispersed homeworkers were easier to lay off in the slumps than a more inflexible factory labour force.

In fact these alternative advantages in dispersed domestic manufacture also help to explain the enigma that once the factory system had appeared as the great novelty on the industrial landscape, it actually spread rather slowly. To be sure, there were striking examples of large-scale factories, not just in the cotton industry but in some silk mills from early in the eighteenth century. There was a Derby silk mill visited in 1719 by Arthur Young, who described it as containing 'machinery driven by a wonderful maze of gearings, in which 26,586 wheels and 97,746 movements were all fed by one large waterwheel'. It employed 200 hands and turned out enormous quantities of silk yearly. This was a celebrated but not an isolated case: there was also one Joseph Stell who converted a fulling mill at Keighly into a silk mill driven by water power 'where he wove tapes, ribbons etc. until he met an untimely end for counterfeiting coins'.[17]

In spite of the well-known examples of the factory, artisan production in small workshops and manufacture in the home organised under the putting-out system were equally important and numerically more significant ways of organising industrial production throughout the Industrial Revolution. Small and medium-sized workshops dominated the metal, hardware and engineering trades throughout the eighteenth and nineteenth centuries, and these were innovative and dynamic enterprises. The putting-out system was widespread in the textile industries until the mid nineteenth century. Under this arrangement merchants or factors provided credit, raw materials and sometimes tools to workers in their own homes, who then produced a finished article within a set time in return for an agreed price per piece. This system, relying on the advantages of cheap dispersed home workers, sometimes developed, as in the stocking knitting industry, into the classic alternative to the factory – sweating. Early knitters were classic peasant workers, combining three or four

2.4. Wensleydale
knitters, by George
Walker (from *The
Costume History of
Yorkshire*, 1814)

days at their knitting frame with farming. But soon large bag hosiers
rented frames to dispersed rural workers, similar in their poverty,
intensive labour and dependence to the sweated clothing workers of
late nineteenth-century London. By 1816 Hayne and Co. had 1000
frames working up to 16 miles from the town. Choice of one
organisation did not exclude the other. The cotton industry combined
examples of widespread putting-out networks with cases of large-scale
factories. In 1791 merchants in Glasgow were employing 15,000
handloom weavers. The calico-printers, Livesay, Hargreaves and Co.
of Blackburn, employed 700–1000 workers before going bankrupt in
1788, and the early socialist Robert Owen accumulated his wealth in
his New Lanark mill which in 1816 was employing 1600–1700
workers. Against such cases of dichotomy between home worker and
huge factory, the norm was small – workshop, home and even factory.
Most of the factories that did exist, even in the cotton industry and
even as late as 1840, were small firms: the average in Manchester was
less than 260 workers and one-quarter employed fewer than 100.

III   Images of improvements and perceptions of new technology

If, as argued above, the Industrial Revolution did not bring such a
sharp break with the pre-industrial rural past as we have previously

thought, was this the way people experienced and perceived it at the time? Certainly, just as there was no single once and for all shift in the organisation of production, so there was no single response to new technologies. The inventions of the Industrial Revolution were not simply large-scale machines and new power sources such as the steam engine; they were new hand-operated tools, new materials and new methods of processing them. The complexities of invention itself were reflected in people's responses. Celebration of novelty was one reaction, and the new industrial towns and country mills – the museums of the future – were incorporated into the Grand Tour of the gentry and middle classes. The Ironbridge of today is a re-creation of those images. But for the people who lived through those transformations in production, however small they may now appear to us, experiences ranged from outright resistance from the earliest days of industrialisation to active worker participation. The artisan inventor was part of the framework of Birmingham's industrialisation, based as it was on hand tools and small machines to aid rather than to displace the skilled worker. Now when we agonise over the social and employment impact of the new micro-electronic technology, it is hard to imagine a precedent. Yet worker resistance to machinery was one of the major problems of the Industrial Revolution. All the major textile innovations of the eighteenth and early nineteenth century were met by waves of machine-breaking. The early mechanisation of the woollen industry in Wiltshire and Somerset at least was carried out under the shadow of the protection of the military. The cotton industry did not escape. Resistance to the jenny and the mule in the eighteenth century was followed by powerloom breaking in the

2.5. Industrial unrest: an attack on the flying shuttle

nineteenth century. Samuel Bamford described an attack on Burton and Sons mill at Middleton in 1812: amongst the rioters were two sisters 'who might have been taken for young amazons so active were they in the pillage and so influential in directing others'. They were known as Clem and Nan, the two tall, dark-haired and handsomely formed daughters of a venerable old weaver who lived on one of the borders of the township.[18]

This resistance of new technology was endemic to British industrialisation, but it was not unique to Britain. Confrontations over machinery were equally part of the heritage of the American and French labour movements. In France the destruction of the spinning jenny was a political act. A recent historian has written that on 13 July 1789 as cannonshot and rifle fire echoed through the Place de la Bastille in Paris, 150 kilometres away in Rouen crowds of women set fire to a pile of wooden jenny parts and watched them burn.[19]

Worker resistance to machinery became, in the early nineteenth century, a more widespread public debate on the directions and social impact of industrialisation itself. Parliament in 1819 and 1820 undertook a public inquiry into the impact of steam engines and furnaces and public health, but never took any positive action on the

2.6. Industrial unrest: a factory destroyed

enormous social and regional divisions created by industrialisation.

Britain's industrialisation found its roots and much of its character in the social structures and production processes already there in pre-industrial rural society. These produced its labour forces, finance and entrepreneurs. Continuities with this past coloured the enormously varied industrial organisations of the eighteenth and nineteenth centuries. But for those who picked up the opportunities or alternatively suffered the destruction of their trades and communities, the transformation of this past as well as building upon it went deep. Within a lifetime, the youth of the eighteenth century had passed from some reasonable knowledge of their future prospects to the great uncertainty of possible prosperity or the despair of the workhouse. Our own anxieties and ambivalence over industrial change can be no greater than those of our forebears. The nineteenth-century Dundee factory boy summed up their feelings:

> The great mass of men and women are like corks on the surface of a mountain river, carried hither and thither as the current may lead them.[20]

Further reading

Maxine Berg, *The Age of Manufactures* (London, 1985); Roy Porter, *English Society in the Eighteenth Century* (Harmondsworth, 1982); Keith Snell, *Annals of the Labouring Poor* (Cambridge, 1985).

CHAPTER THREE	# From Retribution to Reform

Boyd Hilton

3.1. The nineteenth-century view of Heaven

It is common nowadays to talk about 'Victorian values', signifying thrift, hard work, independence, decency and respectability. Yet the concept is rather a surprising one since Queen Victoria reigned from 1837 until 1900, and it seems unlikely that in such a rapidly changing society as nineteenth-century Britain any single system of values could have persisted unchanged for so long. In fact, far from there having been any overall Victorian values, historians tend to distinguish between early, middle and late Victorian periods. This chapter considers the cultural revolution which occurred between the early Victorianism of the 1830s and 1840s and the mid Victorianism of the 1850s and 1860s, especially as it affected religious thought and social policy.

We often think of the 1850s and 1860s as an 'age of doubt' because of the well known 'crises of faith' which many members of the Victorian intelligentsia underwent at that time. It is well known that the truth of Genesis and other large tracts of the Bible was being called into question by geologists, biologists, literary critics and historians. However, we cannot understand the 'spirit of an age' by looking at what a handful of intellectuals thought, and what is clear is that, among the middle and upper classes at least, nineteenth-century British culture was (and remained) overwhelmingly religious.

However, to say that Victorian England was religious is not to say very much. Many societies are. The question is, in what way was it religious? The main characteristic of British people in the first half of the nineteenth century was their preoccupation with Providence – that is, with how God acts in the world. Take, for example, their response to what was undoubtedly one of the greatest natural disasters of the century – the Irish potato famine, which struck in 1845 and for the next four seasons and which killed more than a million Irishmen. The

Great Famine is mainly remembered as a landmark in the development of Irish nationalism, but how about the reaction in the rest of Britain? Nearly everyone agreed that the event was providential. 'Here is a calamity *legibly* divine!' wrote Gladstone to his wife, meaning that one could read God's handwriting in it. 'There is', he went on, 'a total absence of secondary causes which might tempt us to explain it away', meaning that it must be a deliberate act of the Almighty and not merely the consequence of physical laws, such as unfavourable weather patterns or backward methods of agriculture.[1] But what was the message? *Why* should God cause a million Irishmen to starve? For many Englishmen the answer was simple: God had turned on the Irish because of what the English had long considered to be their fecklessness and sloth, their neglect of so-called Victorian values. This was the view of Sir Charles Trevelyan, under-secretary of state in charge of famine relief, who did very little to help Ireland in the crisis because he was reluctant to interfere with market forces, believing as he (and many other people) did that market forces merely manifested God's moral providence. Others pointed to the British government's decision to increase the amount of state subsidy to the Roman Catholic College at Maynooth just months before the famine struck. God was of course assumed to be a Protestant, and many people thought that he must have been so angry at the government's concession to the Irish Catholics that he decided to blight the very next potato crop. But then there were others, less complacent, who feared that the warning must be pointed at England. Irishmen who starved were the lucky ones for they would be whisked to Paradise. It was the English, luxuriating in a railway boom and enjoying unexampled prosperity, who should tremble at what was obviously a warning to them to mend their ways. 'Ireland is the minister of God's retribution', said Gladstone – not the *object* but the *minister*; England was the *object* of God's wrath, and it was essential that Englishmen atone before it was too late.

This sense of retribution, propagated from pulpits up and down the land, also permeated the highest levels of government. Take the home secretary, Sir James Graham, Peel's right-hand man, whom we often think of as a cool and detached administrator. When the first intimations of famine came in October 1845, Graham wrote Peel a long and fairly humdrum letter about the reports he had received, and ended it with the following lament:

It is awful to observe how the Almighty humbles the pride of nations. The Sword, the Pestilence, and Famine are the instruments of his displeasure; the Canker-worm and the Locust are his Armies; he gives the word; a single Crop is blighted, and we see a nation prostrate, and stretching out its Hands for Bread. These are solemn warnings, and they fill me with reverence; they proclaim with a voice not to be mistaken, that 'doubtless there is a God, who judgeth the earth'.[2]

Graham's view may seem wildly apocalyptic to us but at the time it was commonplace. Yet strangely, when – ten years later – the executors of Sir Robert Peel set about publishing that statesman's memoirs and correspondence, they came to Graham's letter and, after a great deal of agonising, decided not to print that concluding paragraph all about God's retribution. They felt that it would offend people's sensibilities to describe the Almighty as a vengeful Old Testament tyrant who would deliberately inflict pain to teach mankind a moral lesson. Reluctantly Graham agreed – which is why the passage has been omitted from the published version of the letter.[3]

For in the Church of England, that is in comfortable upper- and middle-class circles, the image of God was changing – from that of a fierce headmaster proclaiming that vengeance was his – to that of a sort of Santa Claus. There was a famous incident in 1853 when Frederick Denison Maurice was dismissed from his professorship at King's College, London, for daring to suggest that there was no Hell, meaning no place where the damned were literally roasted and tormented for eternity. Twenty, even ten, years later he would have kept his job. By then it would have been widely accepted in Church of England circles that Hell was either a temporary reformatory – the place for a short sharp spiritual shock which would fit a sinner eventually for Heaven – or else a state of nothingness, a void. At the same time men's image of Heaven also turned about. Earlier it had been pictured in the same exaggerated way as Hell, as a place of jewelled pagodas and hallelujah choruses. But then, as the literal image of Hell receded, so Heaven began to be domesticated, came to be seen in terms of a cosy fireside where saints would be surrounded by their long-lost loved ones and by all mod cons and creature comforts. Instead of attempting to terrorise sinners into Heaven, Anglican ministers now placed more emphasis on trying to tempt them thither by promising them more of the good things which they had enjoyed throughout life.

Again, in the 1850s and 1860s people's idea of Jesus changed. In the first half of the nineteenth century it had been the bleeding lamb, the Atonement – Christ's death on the Cross – that signified, because it was believed that a person could enter Heaven *only* if he or she had faith that Jesus had died to save mankind. Mankind had sinned against God in the persons of Adam and Eve, and God had had to exact punishment for that offence, but he had sent his son to bear that

3.2. The altar piece of All Saints Church, Margaret Street, London: Christ on the cross

3.3. Christ in Majesty

punishment in man's place. The Atonement of Christ was therefore called 'the trick of redemption' or 'the scheme of salvation', because it was seen as a mechanism to get believers into Heaven. So the divinity of Christ was the very centre-point of religious belief in the first half of the nineteenth century, and yet people were not actually very interested in what Christ had said and done while he was a man, or in his teaching as it is related in the New Testament.

All this changed in the middle of the century. There was a sudden surge of disgust at the very idea of Atonement, at the notion of a supposedly loving God inflicting pain on the innocent Christ merely in order to get his own back on wicked men. Instead people began to be fascinated with the *life* of Christ, as is clear from the thousands of biographies which began to be written after 1860. The parables as related by Christ, and his various other injunctions on how to behave, to turn the other cheek or love one's neighbour or be a Good Samaritan, all aspects of his ministry which had previously been played down, suddenly came into prominence. Anglican christianity now put over a more gentle, caring conception of the world, and Christmas – a festival celebrated so warmly in the novels of Dickens, for example – replaced Easter as the centre-point of the christian year. The Incarnation, or Christ's becoming man, rather than his death and Atonement, now seemed to be the important thing.

If we have to use labels – and they are always misleading – we would say that the religion of the first half of the century was

3.4. Victorian Christmas celebrations

predominantly 'evangelical'. It assumed that man is inherently sinful, in need of redemption, which is nevertheless open to him if he makes the right choice. The earth is a place of trial, in which God tempts us, tests us, and decides which of us will go to Heaven and which to Hell. God has no other interest in the world except as a sorting ground of future saints and sinners. The religion of the second half of the century, on the other hand, was of a predominantly 'liberal' New Testament sort. God wishes us to make earth as much like Heaven as possible, and so he sent Jesus down among us, not just to be a sacrificial offering but to guide and show us how to make a Heaven on earth. This is why Jesus came to be regarded by many members of the Labour movement in the later nineteenth century as 'the first socialist'.

So in all these ways the idea of a just but savage Jehovah was abandoned in favour of a God who was presumed to stand for gentleness and peace. There was a parallel development in the way in which scientific understanding of the universe changed at this time. During the first half of the nineteenth century scientific thought had been dominated by what we call 'catastrophism'. It derived partly from geology and palaeontology, which were extremely popular and fashionable sciences at the time. By banging around with their hammers, geologists had begun to discover an enormous catalogue of earth history – layers on layers of rock and fossil remains. Yet it was still assumed, on the basis of the Old Testament's genealogical lists, that the earth could only be a few thousand years old. They therefore needed a theory of the earth's formation whereby a great many events could be supposed to have occurred in a very short time-span, and that of course inclined them to believe in catastrophes – in sudden formations and changes – in volcanoes, earthquakes, floods (like Noah's Flood of the Bible), and miracles of that sort. This view of the physical world neatly complemented men's sense of an active God 'who judgeth the earth'.

But in the second half of the century, building on ideas which originated with Sir Charles Lyell, and freed from the constraints imposed by a biblical time-span, geologists came to accept that the earth had developed gradually and, as it were, gently over millions of years. The same applied to life itself, for developments in biological thought, particularly the rapid spread of evolutionary ideas in the mid century, ideas which we particularly associate with the name of Charles Darwin, paralleled the changes in geological thought. Life was no longer seen as arising from some mysterious force or ether which God had manufactured, but was rather the result of long organic development and fruition. Similar views revolutionised physics at the same time; an idea of the continuity or conservation of energy replaced the former notion which had seen the world as being held in equilibrium by external, divinely-ordained forces. In all these ways, men's understanding of the physical and organic world was revolutionised, at the same time as their conception of other-worldly matters was also overturned.

The difficult question is, how do these intellectual currents relate to the state of society and of men's perceptions of it? An obvious point to make about the first half of the century, when catastrophism dominated both science and religion, is that it was an age of revolutions: actual revolutions all over Europe and anticipated revolution here in Britain. This country might be wealthy as never before, but the price of that wealth was the creation of huge cities and a dangerous, downtrodden and explosive proletariat. Because of those insanitary cities it was also an age of epidemics, most notably the terrifying cholera which struck in 1831 and again in 1848. 1831 was just two years after the British Parliament had removed the constitutional restraints on Roman Catholics that went back to the Glorious Revolution of 1688, thereby making Catholics full citizens, and there were many observers who felt sure that the cholera must be a divine punishment for that piece of wickedness, just as there were many who later blamed the famine on the grant to the Catholics of Maynooth. Here is what an evangelical MP called Spencer Perceval (son of the prime minister of the same name) had to say about the cholera from his place in Parliament:

> Will ye not listen for a few moments to one who speaketh in the name of the Lord? I stand here to warn you of the righteous judgment of God, which is coming on you, and which is now near at hand. Ye have in the midst of you a scourge of pestilence, which has crossed the world to reach ye. Ye have mocked God and he will bring on ye fasting and humiliation, woe and sorrow, weeping and lamentation, flame and confusion. I tell ye that this land will soon be desolate: a little time and ye shall howl one and all in your streets.[4]

Perceval was undoubtedly at the extreme end of the evangelical spectrum, his language of lamentation far wilder than most public men would have indulged in, but his basic point – that public and private calamities are always sent by God for a purpose and a chastisement – was one which was very widely shared. After all, the most influential guru of the age was the country vicar Robert Malthus, who at the beginning of the century had prophesied an inevitable cycle of wars, famines and pestilence. This Malthusian prophecy hovered over the imagination of the age like a spectre and came to fulfilment in Ireland in 1845.

Yet, with a suddenness that is difficult to explain, social pessimism evaporated in the 1850s. The ruling classes stopped worrying about revolution, confident that Britain's glorious constitution would satisfy working-class demands. Working men turned away from Chartism, the revolutionary movement of the 1840s, and seemed bent on self-improvement and the peaceful redress of grievances. Malthusian fears about famine suddenly disappeared also as people came to think that we could always import food from the Third World in return for the manufactured goods which we produced. Whereas the 1840s have often been referred to as 'the hungry forties', the fifties and sixties have been called by one famous historian the 'Age of Equipoise', for there was then a sense of calm and content, of improvement, expansion, satisfaction. Perhaps the fact that Britain, alone of the major European nations, had escaped a revolution in the 'year of revolutions', 1848, did much to foster a sense of complacency. Providence was after all, perhaps, on Britain's side.

In terms of social policy too there was a move toward softness, to prevention in place of punishment. The treatment of deviants and social outcasts generally – the poor, the vagrant, the insane, the alcoholic, the child, eventually (though not at once) the criminal – became milder. A good example of this is the changing response to the cholera. In 1831 and 1848 it had seemed to many people impious to try to cure the insanitary condition of the cities. Men had hurried to the towns in search of higher wages, and the wages of their avariciousness had been disease. To try and prevent such providential maladies would be to disturb God's ecological mechanism whereby man was no doubt intended to be forced back to his natural habitat, the morally virtuous countryside. By the 1860s, however, God was no longer thought to operate in such a manner, and men had come to accept the inevitability and even the virtues of industrial life. So when cholera returned in 1866 the response was no longer prayer and fasting but – in Disraeli's phrase – *sanitas sanitatum, omnia sanitas* – the construction of drains and sewers. This was mirrored by changes in medical practice, as a concern for preventive medicine replaced the former cure-all preference for blood-letting, a catastrophic form of treatment which had dominated medical practice in the first part of the century. The most obvious development was in the treatment of the poor, however. The New Poor Law of 1834, with its workhouse test and abolition of outdoor relief, had in theory (though not always in practice) imposed a system of terror and deprivation on the unemployed; by the 1850s the institutions of the Poor Law were being widely used for more generous purposes, for medical and nursing provision and suchlike social kindnesses.

A striking example of this lurch into kindness was the Limited

Liability legislation of 1856. It is fair to point out that if, in the first half of the century, the upper classes had treated the lower classes with harshness, they had at least applied a similar standard to themselves. Many enjoyed enormous wealth but, in that burgeoning capitalist society, much of that wealth was precarious. There were devastating financial collapses – 'commercial earthquakes' or 'mercantile seizures', as they were often called, thus pointing up the geological and medical parallels – in 1825–6, 1837–9, 1847–8 and 1855, when many of the proud and prosperous were humbled overnight, and for such people there was little redress. Shareholders were held liable to their last penny if companies failed and the debtors' prison was to the middle classes what the workhouse was to the poor. It is clear from the novels of the period that the perils of bankruptcy dominated the imagination of the well-to-do.

But in the softer climate of the 1850s the well-to-do decided suddenly to lighten those fears. They allowed themselves to limit their liabilities for debt, so that they would lose only the amount of money which they had personally invested in a failed company. And in doing that, the upper classes chose to soften the capitalist system just at the point where it was hurting themselves. Where it had once seemed right and proper that capital should be spilled from the system every several

3.5. *A Summer Day in Hyde Park*, by John Ritchie (1858)

years, with dire consequences for the victims, of course, just as doctors had thought it right to spill their patients' blood, now the investing upper and middle classes were being invited to seek what profits they might without having to suffer a commensurate penalty when things went wrong. The veteran Scottish political economist John McCulloch had no doubts that this soft-hearted approach to human affairs was an affront to God's righteousness:

In the scheme laid down by Providence for the government of the world, there is no shifting or narrowing of responsibilities, every man being personally answerable to the utmost extent for all his actions. But the advocates of limited liability proclaim in their superior wisdom that the scheme of Providence may be advantage-ously modified, and that debts and contracts may be contracted which the debtors though they have the means, shall not be bound to discharge.[5]

There are obviously many reasons for the change in company law in the 1850s and it would be silly to exaggerate the importance of this moralistic aspect. I would suggest, however, that the capitalist classes chose to soften the capitalist system because they could no longer bear the suspense which that system imposed upon themselves. But this limitation of liability, by making wealth no longer precarious also

3.6. The achievements of British Industry: the Crystal Palace Exhibition Hall

removed what had been one of the major justifications of the capitalist system, which was that the well-to-do gained the rewards but also ran the risks; for those among the well-to-do who were sincere and conscience-stricken, this in turn may have spurred them into taking an equally soft approach to the condition of the lower orders as well.

If this is so, it may provide a clue to what was happening to religion at the same time. It was the middle and upper classes in the established Church of England who decided to abolish Hell in the 1850s and 1860s, or at least to soften its terrors considerably. And of course it was they who had had most cause to be terrified. The poor had always been considered to be in a spiritual sense safe. Just like the Irishmen who starved in 1847, they could be supposed to be bound for Heaven, having suffered so much on earth. But the rich and mighty, those who had not suffered and who had probably succumbed to the tempting snares of earthly wealth, they it was who were mainly bound for that fiery workhouse in the bowels of the earth. The upper classes abolished Hell in the mid century because they could no longer bear the suspense of an evangelical 'scheme of salvation' in which their own chances of victory were meagre. Remember that sin had been thought of in terms of a *ransom* or *debt* which was owed to God and which must be paid if mankind was to be saved; that is why it had made sense to say that Jesus had *redeemed* mankind, for he had by his death and passion *discharged* the debt of sin. In that first capitalist age, it is probably not surprising that the relations between God and man should be conceived in terms of those between creditor and debtor. And that is why it was of central importance when Frederick Denison Maurice, who was, incidentally, a leading supporter of limited liability for investors, boldly denied the reality of Hell. He was (you might say) limiting the liability of sin.

It is impossible to exaggerate the relief which Maurice's new theology brought to the comfortable classes. There were thousands like the society lady whom we read about in the memoirs of Charlotte Williams-Wynn, who had suffered for many years from bouts of acute clinical depression. As Lady Charlotte wrote to Maurice in 1858:

> What religious teaching she had in her youth was of a so called evangelical nature. No sooner did affliction come upon her, than these teachers came about her, wrote, and in short, kept her in a state of high nervous excitement. This will not do for everyday 'wear and tear', and so, though she is loved by all who come near her, and devoted to her poor, she is thoroughly unhappy from the constant fear of the wrath of this inexorable Judge.[6]

But like many others among the ruling classes, this unfortunate lady was apparently cured by Maurice's preaching, in particular by his reassuring assertion 'that God is a God of love, and that He does not punish in anger'.

The point has been made that whereas the old evangelicals had hoped to terrify men into Heaven by threatening them with Hell and the wrath to come, the liberal theologians of the 1850s painted Heaven in a tempting light by domesticating it, so that it could be presented as a continuation of the good things to be enjoyed in life. Obviously, such a strategy could only succeed if life were indeed conceived to be a state of happiness. And this poses a difficulty, which is very common in the history of ideas and attitudes, that it is impossible to tell which came first, the chicken or the egg. Did mid-Victorians respond to social calm and economic prosperity by reorienting their notion of God? Or did a fashionable new system of theology in turn affect their outlook on the world, so that it came to seem a happier and more contented place? Either way, the shift that occurred in the mid century was a profound one indeed.

Further reading

W.L. Burn, *The Age of Equipoise. A Study of the Mid-Victorian Generation* (London, 1964); Colin Chant and John Fauvel (eds), *Darwin to Einstein. Historical Studies on Science and Belief* (London, 1980); Derek Fraser (ed.), *The New Poor Law in the Nineteenth Century* (London, 1976); Walter E. Houghton, *The Victorian Frame of Mind, 1830–1870* (New Haven, 1957); Geoffrey Rowell, *Hell and the Victorians* (Oxford, 1974); G.M. Young, *Portrait of an Age: Victorian England* ed. G. Kitson Clark (Oxford, 1977).

CHAPTER FOUR

The New Babylons

Penelope J. Corfield

I was surprised at the place, but more at the people. They possessed a vivacity I had never beheld. I had been among dreamers, but now I saw men awake. Their every step along the street showed alacrity. Every man seemed to know what he was about.

It was a town that woke the young William Hutton from his slumbers as,[1] like countless other young men and women in eighteenth-century Britain, he left home to make his way in the world. Furthermore, it was a town that was only very small, by modern standards. At the time of Hutton's arrival, in 1741, it housed under 20,000 residents. In other words, it was approximately the same size as modern Stamford; indeed, a prospect of Stamford today shows the newcomer something of the same sight that would have greeted an eighteenth-century migrant: a compact, nucleated, distinctive settlement, with huddled houses, church spires, and a promise of people – and things going on. It was separate and distinct from the surrounding countryside: location and venue for the urban 'way of life'.

The particular town that so galvanised William Hutton was therefore still relatively small (albeit in a much smaller total population) but it was already notable for its activity and dynamism. His secular conversion to modernity in fact occurred in the streets of Britain's new metalware metropolis. 'When the word *Birmingham* occurs', he later confided, 'a superb picture instantly expands in the mind: which is best explained by the other words, grand, populous, extensive, active, commercial – and humane.' When he wrote that, he was not trying to show off an urban sense of humour, but was expressing the sense of both power and civic destiny that was associated with prospering urbanism.[2] Needless to say, not everyone agreed with him. Jane Austen's snobbish Mrs Elton, for one, did not share this enthusiasm. 'One has not great hopes for Birmingham', she observed. 'I always say, there is something direful in the sound.'

Towns, then, could be seen as places of menace, as well as centres of opportunity and dynamism. Indeed, the two reactions were often different sides of the same coin. Opportunity for some was affront or danger to others. Towns were places of challenge, of contest, of ambition. They have – of course – a long history, and have for as long been controversial. Their challenging tradition stretches at least back to mythic Babylon: in Revelations, 'Babylon the Great, the mother of harlots and all the abominations of the earth'. It was matched by the Book of Genesis's depiction of the Tower of Babel, representing the pride as well as the folly of human endeavour, and whose destruction led to the babble of many tongues, the diversification of many cultures. Breughel later painted a magnificently brooding vision of Babel, conveying simultaneously the grandeur and the lurking danger, as urban aspirations reached literally for the skies.

4.1. *The Tower of Babel*, by Breughel

In other words, towns provoked strong reactions, as they do to this day. The urban size and mass, the congregation of many people, imply a potential force or power that may attract or repel. No wonder that governments (and by no means only those in pre-democratic eras) have often been nervous of large cities. But, in these debates, it is important to remember that there was – and is – a pro-town tradition, as well as one of fear or hostility. The existence of 'urban problems' has become too much of a cliché that conceals also urban challenge and power.

In eighteenth-century Britain, many of these viewpoints were urgently canvassed. It was a period of rapid urbanisation, and new Babylons seemed to be springing up on all sides. Criticisms were often voiced in the sternest of moral terms. For one author, the towns were visible embodiments of *Hell-upon-Earth*, no more than one step away from perennial perdition. Hogarth's celebrated attack upon *Gin Lane*, in a print dating from 1751, depicted a searing townscape of universal drink, dissipation, degradation, destruction and death.[3] The scene was a dynamic one, but the energy was demonic, apocalyptic. Amidst the general despair, only Killman the Distiller and Gripe the Pawn-broker flourished.

So powerful was the horror of this classic print, that no wonder moralists shuddered to think that thousands of country people were voluntarily migrating to towns, to join these scenes of desolation. Yet that was not the only verdict upon the urban experience.

Hogarth himself offered an alternative view. *Gin Lane* was, after all, a propaganda piece, as part of the (successful) campaign to regulate the sales of spiritous liquor. It was therefore paired with a companion print, entitled *Beer Street*. This time the positive joys of town life and social drinking were joyously celebrated. Here, the energies were all constructive: houses were built, streets paved, traffic teamed, artists were thriving, songs sung, and much beer drunk. Only Pinch the Pawn-broker was suffering, and even he was allowed a drink through the peep-hole in his boarded-up front door.

For some, therefore, towns were places of conviviality, company, even civility, as Hutton had emphasised. They were places where people had to learn to live together in large numbers. Urban manners and style set the pace, 'urbanity' and 'civility' being terms of strong approval. Furthermore, towns were represented as places of fabled opportunity and adventure, bright lights and bustle: 'where all the streets are paved with gold, and all the maidens pretty'. Of course, this tradition was also much exaggerated and no doubt many eager new arrivals, fresh from the countryside, found the realities much less glamorous. Yet it is important to remember how vital and lively the towns appeared, particularly in the period before mass urbanisation, when town life was the exception rather than the norm. Before the advent of universal electricity, urban settlements were very literally also centres of light. With their illuminated houses and the smart new oil-fired street lamps,[4] the towns stood out as beacons by night, in contrast to the surrounding darkness. They held out both a real and a symbolic promise of enlightenment and man-made power.

'Rusticity' had, by contrast, less pleasant connotations. At best, it denoted a naïve simplicity, at worst a doltish ignorance. 'Is there a creature in the whole country, . . . that does not take a trip to town

4.2. *Gin Lane*, by Hogarth

4.3. *Beer Street*, by Hogarth

now and then, to rub off the rust a little?' enquired a plaintive heroine, fearing the corrosive effect of rural life. 'In my time, the follies of the town crept slowly among us', snapped her elderly husband in reply: 'but now they travel faster than a stagecoach.'[5] The new speed of transport and communications encouraged the spread of information about urban life-styles, accelerating pressures for change.

However much the physical countryside was admired – and town travellers were usually ready to be rapturous – admiration did not often extend to the ordinary residents of rural Britain. They were sneered at as 'country bumpkins' or 'country clowns'. By no means everyone hankered after rural tranquillity. For some, it constituted instead monotony and torpor. 'I have no relish for the country', sighed a worldly parson, who could not find an urban ministry: 'It is a kind of healthy grave.'[6] And many others used this sort of terminology. Rurality was referred to as a state of hibernation or slumber, whereas it was the towns that were eye-opening and full of life.

Little wonder, then, in eighteenth-century Britain that thousands joined William Hutton in his enthusiasm for urban dynamism. Towns were growing rapidly in these years, attracting many visitors and also permanent migrants from the countryside. Few were completely unaffected by the new social magnets. Ordinary country-dwellers took their business into the local market-towns, where they caught up with the news and current affairs of the day. Meanwhile, upper-class landowning families lived, it is true, for part of the year in their grand and gilded country houses. Yet they too joined the stampede to town. The winter social seasons in London and the provincial capitals were thronged with gentry and nobility, as were the emergent summer seasons at the spas and holiday resorts. There, the 'country gentry' rubbed their more or less reluctant shoulders with the newly-confident 'town gentry'. The City of Bath was a notable social meeting-ground. Smollett's crusty Squire Bramble complained that its celebrated 'fashionable company' consisted of 'a very inconsiderable proportion of genteel people, . . . lost in a mob of impudent plebeians'.[7] And, while he exaggerated his case, he identified its social mix as part of the attraction that made Bath one of the most rapidly growing urban places in the whole of Britain.

Most towns, indeed, required an inflow of migrants for sustained population expansion. The crowded streets, teeming houses, often noxious industries, and grossly inadequate town cleansing and sanitation meant that urban mortality levels were chronically high. Paradoxically, while the countryside was denounced by its critics as a 'healthy grave', urban Britain was silently the reverse: socially vital but medically dangerous. That, however, did not enter into the pro-town mythology. Plainly, too, it did not stop the sustained migration

4.4. The Royal Exchange in the late eighteenth century

from the countryside.[8] Some of those moving were themselves victims of agrarian change, pushed off the land. But that did not necessarily dictate an urban destination. It was possible to move to other parts of the countryside, or to emigrate overseas – as indeed quite a number did. Yet there was also a positive attraction from the towns, as people moved there in search of jobs, of social amenities, and a myriad of opportunities that were not available in traditional rural society.

Women were particularly notable in the quest for urban liberation. Country life was very much more of a male preserve, dominated by male values and masculine occupations and pursuits. In towns, by contrast, social networks were more open and diversified, although they were by no means havens of matriarchy. The many references to women's eagerness to flee the countryside were probably exaggerated, but they pointed to a real social trend. Eighteenth-century plays and poems made much of this as a stock theme. Sheridan's Lady Teazle leaves the *School for Scandal* – which was the chatterbox city itself – with the deepest forebodings:

> In a lone, rustic hall for ever 'pounded,
> With dogs, cats, rats, and squalling brats surrounded,
> With humble curate can I now retire,
> While good Sir Peter boozes with the squire.[9]

And, earlier, Alexander Pope had penned a truly superb lament for a young lady's unwilling departure from town:

> She went – to plain-work and to purling brooks,
> Old-fashion'd halls, dull aunts, and croaking rooks;
> She went – from Opera, park, assembly, play,
> To morning walks; and prayers three times a day.
>
> To pass her time, 'twixt reading and Bohea*;
> To muse, and spill her solitary Tea;
> And o'er cold coffee trifle with her spoon,
> Count the slow clock – and dine exact at noon.[10]

(* black China tea)

Rooks, parsons and elderly relatives were often taken as emblematic of rustic society, which was, of course, a little unfair; but it helps to set the mood of the times. Certainly it was the case that all eighteenth-century towns, for which detailed evidence has survived, showed a majority of women among their resident populations. That was partly as a result of female longevity, but partly too an indication of their participation in the townward migration.

Some of these optimists were particularly at risk as they first made their way in town society. Young country girls were much in demand as domestic servants: so much so that experienced city misses were not above leaving town in order to return in the marketable guise of country newcomers. But city sharks were notoriously ready to prey upon these unwary novices, in the interests of an even older profession.[11] Bawds and procurers lay in wait at the coaching inns, ready to tempt with false offers of accommodation and employment. The *Harlot's Progress*, as depicted by Hogarth, began in such a way. Scene One was set in the yard of the Bell Inn, where the York wagon had just arrived. The country miss was fresh-faced, with a rose at her breast and a goose in her basket. She was unwittingly inspected by a notorious brothel-keeper, herself richly dressed but pockmarked and worldly. Meanwhile, an unlovely client lurked nearby, all too visibly; and, uncaring, town life went on all round, as a woman hung out her washing and a myopic parson rode by.

That was a sharp reminder – if one was needed – that not all urban adventures turned out well. The first lesson for newcomers was to keep their wits about them. Hazards were everywhere. Initial impressions of busy town life could be completely overwhelming, producing the 'town shock' that is still felt by some newcomers to this day. Often noted by eighteenth-century visitors was the pace and bustle of it all. People moved around rapidly, and modern studies have interestingly confirmed that, the larger the town, the faster the mean pace of peregrination. In 1771, Smollett again waxed sardonic on the crowds in London, already a great 'world city' and therefore a place of very speedy citizens:

> All is tumult and hurry; [and] one would imagine they were impelled by some disorder of the brain, that will not suffer them to be at rest. The foot passengers run along as if they were pursued by baillifs; the porters and chairmen trot with their burdens.[12]

The general noise and bustle and activity could prove highly disconcerting to newcomers, when everyone else seemed to have something to do and to know where to go. 'I felt uneasy and helpless in the middle of an immense town, of which I did not know a single street', confided an American visitor in 1810.[13] (His solution was to jump into a hackney cab.) Yet another celebrated traveller to Manchester meditated, in a similar vein: 'A feeling of melancholy, even uneasiness, attends our first entrance into a great town, especially at night. ... The sense of all this vast existence, ... where we are utterly unknown, oppresses us with our insignificance.' That was from the pen of the not-easily-cowed young Disraeli in 1844. After further urban exploration, he was moved to assert that: 'The Age of Ruins is past!' Which he explained with the assessment that 'Rightly understood, Manchester is as great a human exploit as Athens!'

There were, however, many ways of coping with the initial town

4.5. The stage coach to Town

shock. For the literate, there was a fast-growing literature of interpretation: guide-books, handbooks, directories, local topographical surveys. And for all comers, the coaching inns seem to have acted as unofficial clearing-houses. They helped people to find housing close at hand and regional clusters of country migrants were often found to have settled around these transport termini – just as later their successors did around the great Victorian railway stations. When in 1794 Godwin wrote his tense melodrama of flight and pursuit, he imagined his fugitive hero in hiding in London. *Caleb Williams* choses an obscure hostelry in Southwark, 'chosing that side of the metropolis on account of it lying entirely wide of the part of England from which I came.' His grim pursuer, meanwhile, tracks him down by asking patiently from inn to inn.[14]

Migrants, even in flight, were less alone than they appeared, or felt themselves, to be. Sometimes artisan clubs and trade societies provided travellers with letters of introduction to others in the same line of business. Some churches did the same for their own membership. Networks of contacts – regional, familial, religious, economic – softened the shock of the move. The private Catholic chapels played that role for the growing numbers of Irish migrants into British towns. Meanwhile there were, for example, many Welsh-speaking churches in London, Manchester and Birmingham. Also there flourished a myriad of special clubs and societies: there was a Scots Society in Norwich, and a Norwich Society in London. Town networks were complex and interlocking. At the same time, it is worth remembering that some people also enjoyed the relative freedoms and anonymity that urban life made available. Much the best place to be alone, averred Addison in 1711, was amongst the heart of the crowds in a large city.[15]

Certainly, towns were not simply anarchic jungles, without reason or structure. On the contrary, they were marvels of organisation and complexity. Especially so, as their early expansion was unpremeditated and unplanned. By the end of the eighteenth century, Britain's urban population amounted to almost 3 million people, in a total population of three times that.[16] Since the townees did not till the land and produce their own foodstuffs, it took an immensely productive agrarian system, as well as a fast and efficient trade and transport network, to feed their growing numbers and to supply their industries with raw materials. Roads, rivers, sea-lanes and canals bustled with activity. There was also an important reverse flow, from the towns outwards to the surrounding countryside. Goods and services were produced by urban workforces, for both urban and rural consumers. Towns were not parasites. Instead, their own expansion stimulated wider economic growth. That was noted by Adam Smith, among others. In *The Wealth of Nations* (1776), he devoted a key chapter to a full analysis of 'How the Commerce of the Towns contributed to the Improvement of the Country'.[17]

After a long century of strong trading and colonial expansionism, it was not surprising that Smith's attention was concentrated initially upon urban commerce. Already, however, towns were important for a notable diversity of economic functions. The sprawling London conurbation itself very visibly embodied a pluralism of role. As capital city, it housed the headquarters of government and monarchy. 'Legal London' clustered around the Inns of Court, while 'Theatrical London' thrived in Covent Garden, which was simultaneously the location for a notorious red light area. 'Fashionable London' spread westwards; 'criminal' London flourished – by repute at least – in crowded St Giles parish; 'financial and banking London' stayed put in the traditional 'City'. Meanwhile, there were docklands along the river to the east, and numerous industrial suburbs, such as silk-weaving Spitalfields. Its diversity was made up of countless urban specialisms.[18] Very much the same pattern was seen, too, among the fast growing towns of provincial Britain. Here different places had their own specialisms. Ports and markets dealt with the distribution of goods and services, while spas and holiday resorts were centres for conspicuous consumption plus medical attention (a spartan British combination). Some cloistered Barchesters focused upon cathedral and clerical services. Dockyard towns, like Portsmouth and Plymouth, meanwhile, housed the specialist workforces that built and maintained the country's naval defences. Above all, a multiplying tribe of manufacturing towns produced a multiplying range of consumer goods, for both export and domestic markets. Celebrated centres of industrial Britain – Manchester, Birmingham, Sheffield, Leeds – were already large and fast-growing in the eighteenth century.[19] Indeed, with the obvious exception of the later railway towns, virtually all the major towns of Victorian Britain were established as places of urban significance under the Hanoverians.

Vigorous expansion was reflected in the general building and rebuilding that was apparent on all sides. Old-style plasterwork and thatch was replaced by modish brick and tile. Streets and crescents proclaimed a fashionable new urban style and layout. Theatres, assembly-rooms and town halls sprang up, even in the smallest towns. Tiny Stamford, for example, had acquired all three, at a time when its resident population was little more than 4000 individuals. Of course, while urban growth as a whole was not planned or anticipated – mass urbanisation was a new phase in human history – individual patrons and promoters joined in with enthusiasm. The Lowthers, a Cumbrian landowning family, sponsored the growth of the port of

Whitehaven, building a neat grid-iron of slate-grey housing under the shelter of St Bee's Head. Famously, too, the great urban show-case city of Bath had some important promoters. The John Woods – senior and junior – constructed a fluent townscape for social parade and display, while Richard 'Beau' Nash simultaneously instructed its clientele in the niceties of gracious living. But sponsorship did not always work the trick. A number of people burned their fingers trying to develop resorts that did not achieve fashionable success.[20] The London hatter, Sir Richard Hotham, for example, spent over £60,000 in the 1780s and 1790s, trying to promote the seaside hamlet he named after himself as 'Hothampton'. He failed, and only several decades later did the resort achieve a decorous success – and a change of name – as Bognor Regis.

Those places that were growing – and they were plentiful – therefore had a viable economic base. Their successful expansion tended to produce in their populations an attitude of pride, and independence from external controls. They were hard-working, busy places, full of the confidence in growth that is found in the innocent early days of expansionism. There was an almost tangible sense of the forging of a new urban culture. Songs, ballads, and popular tales helped to assimilate change.[21] 'Sheffield's a Wonderful Town O', ran one local refrain. 'Shrewsbury for me!' countered another. 'O the brave Dudley boys', sang a protest march of Dudley colliers. Identities were also expressed in satire and mockery, both in print and ballad. Towns were testing societies, ready to challenge complacency. 'Manchester's improving daily' was sung with heavy sarcasm; and the *Barnsley Anthem* satirised its urban muck:

> If bum bailiffs come,
> They nivver will find us –
> 'Cos we're all dahn in t'cellar 'oil*
> Wheer muck slaght† on t'winders.
> (* hole)   († dashes)

Yet there was familiarity, even affection, amidst the laughter. Satire was a distinctly knowing form of communication, depending upon the quick-witted urban audiences' readiness to get the jokes, which the country bumpkins (at least in the townsmen's estimation), always failed to understand.

Confidence in city ways therefore meant that urban problems were deemed matters to be tackled in their urban context. For there were undoubtedly problems in modern Babylon, as Hogarth and many others had pointed out. Putting a lot of people together on one site had immediate implications for housing, water supply, sanitation, refuse collection, social amenities, education, policing: all the classic issues that still constitute much of the staple business of urban local government to this day.

Certainly, as some towns grew particularly rapidly, their environments deteriorated. Gardens and orchards were built over and housing densities shot up. Within two generations, for example, Nottingham had changed from being an agreeable, leafy county capital of some fame, into a warren of back-to-back housing in enclosed yards, entered only by narrow alleyways, all of some notoriety.[22] Its problems were particularly acute, as it was surrounded by enclosed land and unable for some decades to grow outwards. But many towns had poor areas, earlier known as 'rookeries' (which was perhaps too rural a metaphor) and later renamed as 'slums' – a slang term, extending from its original meaning of low-class rooms, to endorse entire districts of bad housing.

In some manufacturing towns, too, the early factories that provided work for new migrants also provided blight, whose full impact took time to recognise and even longer to remedy. Later generations, who

4.6. A nineteenth-century panorama of Manchester

have notably also underestimated the problems in new technologies of power and transport cannot, however, afford to be too condescending to past urban societies. In fact, many towns saw some efforts at improvement. Earliest attention was given to street cleansing and lighting. Sometimes enlightened municipalities took the lead, in other places groups of individuals or private companies. Professional men were active, quite a number of clergymen and many doctors taking an interest in medical reforms; and in Manchester in the 1790s the first local Board of Health was founded by a group of local practitioners. It was all very localised and *ad hoc*. Standards varied immensely from town to town, and certainly also within towns. The resorts all hastened to advertise themselves as highly salubrious, while the most notoriously filthy city of all was ancient Edinburgh, where muck was still thrown into the streets with the traditional cry of 'Gardey-loo' (*gardez-l'eau*).[23] The Georgian patchwork quilt of local initiatives and local diversity, however, provided a basis upon which the Victorian reformers later built, in their own very variable efforts at standardisation of urban reform. In other words, the modern dialectic between municipal and national governments had begun.

The lure of the town had, therefore, many implications that affected society as a whole, as well as the hopeful young migrants who trod in the footsteps of William Hutton. A stereotyped view of eighteenth-century Britain, where an obsequious peasantry stands, endlessly doffing hats to a complacent squirearchy, cannot be substantiated. By the end of the century, at least 1 in 3 people did not live on the land, but in towns, and many more had visited or resided there at some stage or other in their lives. The urban minority was increasingly influential, magnetic. If traditional landowning society (itself, incidentally, a much smaller minority) had its hands upon some traditional levers of political power, then the towns were challenging with new resources of economic wealth, social attraction, and cultural vitality.[24] The system would eventually have to come to terms with its 'populous places', as prime minister Pitt admitted in debate in 1784. Actual political reforms took some time to arrive successfully onto the statute book; yet the power of the urban lobby was already apparent well before the legislative changes of the 1830s. Town pressures were effected directly by municipal leadership and behind-the-scenes campaigning. They were also indirectly sensed, simply through the diverse and often chilling experience of town life itself. The 'cry of the harlot' in the city streets 'shall weave old England's winding sheet', as William Blake's subversive vision prophesied.[25] Within the challenging turmoils of modern Babylon a yet mightier urban Jerusalem beckoned.

Crowds, bustle, noise, quick wits, high hopes and a sharp eye for urban pickpockets were essentials of town life. As more and more people shared the urban experience, so pressures for change mounted. Mass urbanisation has been a long-term revolutionary force whose full implications are not yet concluded. In eighteenth-century Britain, change was represented in the intent hum of the busy market place; in the smoke and clatter of the manufacturing towns; in the swaying masts and laden quaysides of the ports and harbours; in the regimentals of the dockyard towns; in the sauntering promenades at the spas and resorts; in the great 'world-city' of London. 'If I was to entitle ages', observed Horace Walpole in 1761, 'I would call this *the Century of Crowds*'.[26] And there they were, all hurrying into town.

Further reading

C. Chalklin, *The Provincial Towns of Georgian England, 1740–1820* (London, 1974); P. Clark (ed.), *The Transformation of English Provincial Towns, 1600–1800* (London, 1984); P.J. Corfield, *The Impact of English Towns, 1700–1800* (Oxford, 1982); R. Glen, *Urban Workers in the Early Industrial Revolution* (London, 1984); D. George, *London Life in the Eighteenth Century* (London, 1966); L. Mumford, *The Culture of Cities* (London, 1938); G. Simmel, 'Metropolis and Mental Life' in K.H. Wolff (ed.), *The Sociology of Georg Simmel* (Glencoe, Illinois, 1964); J. Walvin, *English Urban Life, 1776–1851* (London, 1984); R. Williams, *The Country and the City* (London, 1973).

CHAPTER FIVE

The Working Classroom

Philip Gardner

In 1851, Henry Hitchcock lived at Number Four, Pope's Parade, in the centre of the city of Bristol. He was 45 years old and earned his living as a labourer in a large iron foundry. He had spent his whole life in the city, but his wife Ann had been born in a tiny Devonshire village in the year 1800. She, along with countless others of her generation, had been attracted from her rural home by the lure of Britain's rapidly growing industrial towns. The Hitchcocks shared Number Four, Pope's Parade with five other labouring families – 21 people in all. It was a dark, squalid and overcrowded place. The building saw many comings and goings, and some of these would have been connected with the little school which, unexpectedly, was kept here.[1]

5.1. Four Pope's Parade, Bristol

In themselves, these are trivial historical facts. But as token of wider historical change, they are very important. Henry Hitchcock's work in the iron foundry; Ann Hitchcock's transition to city life; the family's precarious daily existence in a crowded and changing urban environment: all these marked out an experience of life which was a fundamentally new one for the mass of the British people. It was a life which was being replicated in every town and city in this, the world's first industrial nation. It was a life which was, as the nineteenth century went on, rapidly to become a familiar pattern for millions of unremembered individuals like Henry and Ann Hitchcock. It was, in short, a working-class life.

Many of us might instinctively feel that we know a great deal about these people and their culture. After all, in time and in place, they remain very near to us. We can, for example, witness their names and a few fragments of biographical detail in the long, silent lists of the Population Census returns; we can watch their images staring back at us from the first photographs; we may daily use the very buildings and streets planned and constructed by them; we can recognise them as the creatures of a modern industrial society, as we know ourselves to be. We can read more about them, whether as fact or as fiction, whether in parliamentary Blue Books or in Dickens, than we can of labouring people from any earlier historical time.

We are so close then to the early working class, with a wealth of documentary material to hand. How could we do other than to believe that these are a people, that this is a culture which, historically, we know well? And yet the belief is an illusion.

The things that we do know about them are no more than the bare bones of a working-class existence. The working class, as we understand it, was a product of the social and economic transformation of the late eighteenth and early nineteenth centuries which we commonly know as the Industrial Revolution. Henry Hitchcock and his contemporaries would have been witness to these dramatic and fateful changes: to the harnessing of steam power; to the spread of mechanisation and factory production; to the arrival of the railways; above all, to the draining of population from the countryside of traditional Britain to the expanding towns and cities which pointed the way to an industrial future.

But the Hitchcocks were more than witnesses to such changes. They, like the rest of the new working class, were a living part of the transformation. And it was within an atmosphere of change, dislocation and uncertainty that the Hitchcocks had to live their lives; to earn a steady and sufficient living, to maintain a home, to protect and educate their children, and to defend their personal dignity. In the towns of early nineteenth-century Britain, these were not modest goals. Life for working people was hard and frequently short. Security was elusive.

To support themselves and their families, the growing army of industrial workers found that their sole individual resource was the sale of their labour to the owners of factories, workshops and mines. But for most this resource was, alone, an inadequate one, and in an age before the State welfare provisions of our own century, personal disaster was never far away. But there was another resource to be drawn upon. This was the *shared* resource of the culture which the new class generated; in other words, its way of life. It was a culture given substance by shared individual experiences of hardship and uncertainty. It was a culture given shape by an awareness that mutual self-help brought some measure of collective strength in place of individual weakness. It was a culture which defended and sustained its members in the local settings of everyday life – in the home, in the workplace, in the street, in the schoolroom.

We can identify the existence of this culture: understanding it is a

5.2. Slum dwellings,
Bluegate Fields, London

different problem. One way of gaining an insight into what was a rich and complex way of life is to look at working-class attitudes to education and at the little-known schools they themselves created and financed. This will be an enquiry which, fittingly, will lead us back to our starting place, to the crowded house in Pope's Parade. But this kind of enquiry is never easy, for a number of reasons.

In the first place, we have to recognise that the vast majority of our documentary sources for early working-class culture were seldom the direct products of that culture. They come to us from outside observers. In particular, they come from that influential group of middle-class social investigators characteristically fascinated by the unfolding drama of unprecedented Victorian social change. One of the most obsessive concerns of such writers was the question of the urban working class and its 'improvement'. They were acutely aware that a great new social class was being brought into existence. They knew that they were dependent upon it and yet it also represented a constant threat to them. As for the working-class way of life, this was a considerable puzzle which outside observers found hard to understand. This helps to explain the characteristic tone of so much middle-class writing of the period: a mixture of contempt for the products of working-class culture and optimism for a future in which that culture would be reformed through the efforts of middle-class philanthropy.

For historians, this must be a recognition of paramount importance.

We cannot go on accepting the surface judgements of the Victorian observers wholesale as we have tended to do. Like archaeologists, we cannot be content with studying just the surface remains of history. We will have to excavate at deeper levels to complete a fuller and more accurate historical picture. We will, in other words, have to uncover new historical sources to confirm or to challenge the more familiar evidence. To have the greatest comparative value, such new sources will be those with a relatively neutral character, like the returns of the Population Census, and those which constitute genuinely 'upward' evidence, such as working-class autobiography. Though certainly less convenient to use, such sources can yield rich and illuminating results.

But it is more than just the problem of biased sources which we have to confront. The way in which we respond to such sources is also important. To-day, our lives are heavily influenced by the cultural patterns encouraged by a strong, centralising State. But in the nineteenth century, this was much less the case. Then, the working class had more space to retain and develop its own culture. But, as we have seen, this capacity was viewed 'from above' with fear and suspicion. Nevertheless it seemed as though the potential social dangers could be reduced to some degree by utilising the agencies of an expanding State to remodel working-class culture. The social implications of this process, once set in train, have been – and continue to be – profound. In particular it has come to make it very difficult for us, in the late twentieth century, to understand the extent to which an independent and alternative culture could flourish just a few generations ago. In this sense, we have become intellectually estranged from, and deprived of, what was a genuinely popular cultural inheritance.

Therefore if we are to have any real understanding of early working-class culture, we will have to overcome not just the barrier of biased historical sources but also of our own restricted historical imagination. Let us now attempt to scale these barriers in a practical way. Consider this question: what was the place of education in the cultural life of the early working class? If we consult the social investigations of the nineteenth century and, by extension, the standard modern histories of education, then the answer is straight-forward – virtually no place at all. The impression we gain is that organised learning and working-class culture were, in effect, opposites. We learn that the education of the mass of the population was a benefit which could be supplied only 'from above'. The author of a government report of 1861 expressed this view succinctly:

By no sudden process of self-development has any community ever been known to start from ignorance to knowledge – from brutality to civility. ... The working population has shown no inborn or spontaneous power of self-improvement.[2]

Another writer suggested that education was 'an advantage which they do not appreciate and would in many cases rather be without'.[3] This illustrates a viewpoint from which the landmarks in the development of popular education were laid down by the work of Church and State. And no landmark was so outstanding as the great Education Act of 1870. By this Act, the State finally brought a basic education to all sections of the working class and established an indelible mark on the future development of a national system of education. The 1870 Act thus served to fill an educational void in working-class culture. To do so, it had necessarily to provide for attendance at State-sponsored schools to be made compulsory. Working people would have to be coerced into accepting a benefit for their own good.

But did the void actually exist? There is strong evidence that it did not. For example, the annual report of the Bristol School Board for 1875 catalogued attendance figures of children at the city's State-supported schools. Part of the report read:

The foregoing statistics take no account whatever of the large and constantly fluctuating number of private adventure schools ... which are not considered as affording efficient instruction to the large number of children attending them. ... The number of schools of this class was 160, which were said to be attended by 4,280 scholars.[4]

Further research showed that Bristol was not unique. Working-class private adventure schools flourished throughout the century up to the early 1870s. In many areas, between 30 and 50 per cent of scholars were attending such schools.

The Bristol School Board was certainly not the only one to express irritation at the continuing presence of so many popular private schools. In 1875, more than 200 Boards took part in a systematic campaign of memorials and deputations to the Education Department.[5] They complained of the damaging impact of the private schools on 'efficient' Board schools. The government listened, and obliged. The 1876 Education Act included careful provisions of attendance which, in the words of its author, Lord Sandon, ensured that 'the great majority of the labouring classes will be virtually compelled to send their children to the public elementary schools.'[6] Such publicly supplied schools moved in to take the place of the officially unmourned private schools. But the new schools were *not* moving into a void. They were colonising the territory of a pre-existing popular educational culture. Like most unequal colonial conquests, the triumph of State education was won under the banners of civilisation and national progress. These helped to obscure the reality of a deeply contested cultural struggle. But the private schools were without powerful defenders then, as now. Condemned by 'expert' opinion as worthless and irrelevant, they have been allowed to sink into historical oblivion. However, as we try to pull them back to the centre of the historical stage, we begin to rediscover not only some surprising working-class attitudes to education, but abundant evidence of a practical culture living successfully on its own terms.

What were private adventure schools? What were they like? How were they different from schools provided by the State? What clues can they give us about the culture which produced and shaped them?

In some ways, 'school' is a misleading term here, though it is hard to find a more suitable one. There was never a purpose-built schoolroom. Instead, a cluster of children of all ages – sometimes as few as half a dozen, sometimes as many as fifty – gathered in the kitchen of a neighbour who could teach basic skills in return for a few pence a week. But the absence of specialised buildings is not important. Private adventure schools were a genuine cultural response to a real popular demand for education. This demand was extremely specific in character and had several major elements.

In the first place, the accent was firmly on gaining the basic skills of literacy – especially reading – and not on moral improvement, as in publicly supplied schools. Reading was prized above all as the passport to potentially unlimited knowledge, as a key to unlock any door. More than one contemporary observer was obliged to concede that, in this respect, the private schools responded to demand: 'It is almost the universal opinion of parents that children are taught to read quicker and better [in the private schools] than in the lower classes of the public schools.'[7] This is a judgement frequently supported by autobiographical recollection, like that of Thomas Cooper. His teacher, 'Old Gatty' was, 'an expert and laborious teacher of the art of reading and spelling. . . . I soon become her favourite scholar, and could read the tenth chapter of Nehemiah, with all its hard names . . . and could spell wondrously.'[8]

Beyond this, learning had to be rapid, effective and cheap. Moreover, schooling had to be organised flexibly to fit in with the ups and downs of the family economy and daily patterns of working life. These dictated that attendance at school, for example, could seldom be regular. Children were of necessity not just pupils but also workers – whether domestic or casual – who had to contribute materially to

5.3. Private Venture
Schools

5.4. Private Venture
Schools

5.5. Private Venture
Schools

the family economy. In the private schools, children would come and
go as they would to their own homes, and as the financial situation of
their families permitted. A contemporary magazine article explained
that:

> though . . . nine o'clock . . . is nominally the time at which children
> should come in . . . they are dropping in all morning long . . . while
> it is an hourly occurrence for mother unceremoniously to throw
> open the school door and call out Johnny or Polly to run an
> errand.[9]

Learning would be done when there was an opportunity; teaching
would be mixed with the normal domestic activity and atmosphere of
a family home.

G.R. Porter described one such school in a typical London court of
the 1830s:

> there is a school in the court, attended by about 50 scholars, held in
> a room twelve feet square . . . which is the sole dwelling of the
> schoolmaster, his wife, and six children . . . the mode of payment is
> remarkable and characteristic. A kind of club, which does not
> consist exclusively of the parents of the scholars, meets every
> Saturday evening at a public house; when, after some hours spent in
> drinking and smoking, a subscription is raised and handed over to
> the schoolmaster, who forms one of the company, and who is
> expected to spend a part of the money in regaling the subscribers.[10]

School life then, was indistinguishable from home life. Teachers were
not intruders into the culture. They were as much a product of it as
were their clients. They were neighbours and friends. To education
officials this was highly unsatisfactory. In their view, a professionalised
teaching force administering a measured dosage of formal schooling
was the target. One school inspector wrote scathingly that 'the teacher
of the adventure school has a personal following. She is probably
related to half her neighbours.'[11]

Above all, working-class demand required that their schools should
be directly and minutely responsive to their needs. Time and money
were precious resources which could not be wasted on schools which
did not measure up to demand. There was a necessary cultural
consonance between home and school here which was massively
lacking in the case of the public school and its harassed teachers, as
any perusal of nineteenth-century school log-books is likely to reveal.
A cheap and basic education could certainly be obtained at the State-
aided schools, but in other respects this supply was unsuited to

working-class demand. It was commonly seen as an alien presence: inflexible, imperious and moralistic, as well as irrelevant. The Victorian writer J.G. Fitch reported for example that:

> there are many parents who object to the religious character so strongly impressed upon most of the State-aided schools. I attended a large meeting of working people in Leeds . . . and in the course of the discussion, I asked how it was that . . . so many parents seemed to prefer the private school. One speaker said strongly that for his part he thought 'it was because there was too much religion in the aided schools' and the remark was very loudly and generally cheered.[12]

This then was the nature of working-class demand – cheap, effective, flexible and responsive schooling. The private school was the natural answer: a school entirely outside the regulation or inspection of the State; entirely unaffected by the moral strictures of middle-class philanthropy; entirely under the control and direction of its users. Private schools could do all that working-class culture demanded of them. In the terms of this culture, such schools were highly successful. An individual example was 'Old Betty W's school' in Tunstall in the 1830s. One former pupil, Charles Shaw, later wrote:

> I must have attended her school between three or four years. The school was the only room on the ground floor of her little cottage. The furniture was very scant, consisting of a small table, two chairs, and two or three little forms about eight inches high for the children to sit upon. . . . The course of education given by the old lady was very simple and graded with almost scientific precision. . . . Though she never taught writing, her scholars were generally noted for their ability to read while very young . . . I could read the Bible with remarkable ease when I left her school, when seven years old . . . she was deeply respected by both children and parents.[13]

Though old Betty's teaching was sound, and though her school was popular, both were, in the eyes of education officials, 'inefficient' by their very nature.

Schools like this were everywhere. Private schools were part of the ebb and flow of daily working-class life. They sprang into existence whenever and wherever there was a demand for them. The manner in which the traveller Paul Hawkins Fisher stumbled across such a school in 1870 is quite typical:

> When the writer was on horseback in a part of the Cotteswold range

. . . he dismounted at a cottage to inquire his way; and on opening the door he found it was a school for children. The mistress was walking backward and forward, spinning some wool into yarn and performing her scholastic duties at the same time. A boy was in the act of reading his lesson aloud to her.[14]

And the educationalist George Bartley could write in 1870: 'There is scarcely an alley or court in the crowded districts of London and the larger towns in which such schools may not be found.'[15]

Large cities like Bristol would have been host to many schools like old Betty's. In Henry Hitchcock's day, there were more than 200 such. Indeed, a school was kept at Number Four, Pope's Parade itself, by another resident, Mary Facey. Whatever learning Henry Hitchcock's children managed to gain would almost certainly have come from this close neighbour. The returns of the Population Census usually disclose the only faint documentary mark which these once crowded and bustling little schools have left to history. Schools such as the little 'Cottage School' kept by Harriet Uphill, like so many other teachers, a lone woman, making her own way.[16] She was, nonetheless, an important and valued figure within the local community, as was her near neighbour, Ann Reece, who kept a 'small school for children' just a few streets away.[17] For cities like Bristol, the Population Census reveals scores of little schools like these in working-class districts, serving the population with an informal educational network, with no

5.6. 1851 Census return for Bristol

home being far from a school. Like the schools themselves, most of the buildings which housed them have now been swept away.

To the middle-class observer, this essentially domestic and apparently chaotic provision of schools was a travesty of the true education required for the masses. In the private school, there was no central planning, no formal physical or moral regulation, no fixed teacher-pupil roles, no uniform, no registration, no records, no trained teachers. The very domestic informality which was so attractive to working class users horrified educationists:

'The worst of the private adventure schools,' according to one writer, 'are those in which 30 or 40 children are crowded into the kitchen of a collier's dwelling, and the mistress divides her attention between teaching them, nursing her own baby, and cooking for her husband and sons. In one such school, the collier and two lodgers, just from the pit, were at dinner, and, it is to be feared, afterwards undressed and washed themselves in the same apartment.'[18]

Another writer charted just how far these schools fell short of middle-class ideals:

I have visited schools in which there has been a total absence of all attempt to introduce method or discipline – where constant disorder prevails, and where children are permitted to attend without the slightest regulation as to cleanliness of dress or person.[19]

An official of the Anglical National Society complained that the working class, 'resist the discipline of our schools to a surprising extent; they do not like the obligation of attending at fixed hours, and conforming to rules, having clean dress and short or tidy hair.'[20] These little private schools were different in almost every respect from the much bigger, highly formal State-supported schools, and they were patronised to an extent which the public schools were not. Middle-class philanthropy was mystified and outraged; Nassau Senior complained of, 'these dens of ignorance to which one-third of the labouring classes still send their children . . . although good and cheap public schools are at their doors.'[21]

One of the schools which Senior had in mind was observed by a School Inspector in Rochdale. He reported that he was:

'fortunate in having seen one of the noblest specimens of schools. There could hardly be a more striking sight,' he went on, 'to the understanding eye than the interior of this school, in which I have seen 600 children present at one time, all under the most perfect command, moving with the rapidity and precision of a machine, and learning as though they were learning for their lives.'[22]

The mechanical analogy here was not accidental. Schools like these were designed, in effect, to manufacture a new working-class. But for them to do so effectively, the schools under the control of the old working class would have to be destroyed. This would drive a wedge between parent and child; between the old and the new. As representatives of an unreformed culture, parents, far from being the partners of publicly-supplied schools, became instead their greatest obstacles. Thus could the manager of a Church school in the 1860s complain that:

> Our chief hindrances are the neglect of the parents, in not enabling the children to be punctual, and their evil example, by which, for the most part, the best instruction, and even the most favourable impressions are quickly effaced.[23]

The 'evil example' of parents was complemented by that of the private school. To most observers, such schools were more than mere irritants. They were the living symbols of a squalid, dangerous and stubbornly independent culture which would have to be reformed. This was the aim and the achievement of the educational legislation of the 1870s. By the close of the nineteenth century, working-class private schools were effectively a thing of the past. Whilst the private schools of the rich could continue to boast of their illustrious histories, those of the poor disappeared almost as though they had never been.

In the twentieth century, we have come to see schools provided by the State as the true 'peoples' schools'. Yet history can show us that there were once more authentic claimants to this title: schools growing naturally *from* the people and their culture and not manufactured *for* them by the State. If we are to acknowledge the constructive achievements of State education after the Act of 1870, we would do well to ponder also on that which it destroyed.

Further reading

P. Bailey, *Leisure and Class in Victorian Britain: Rational Recreation and the Contest for Control* (London, 1978); D. Vincent, *Bread, Knowledge and Freedom* (London, 1981); J. Burnett (ed.), *Destiny Obscure* (London, 1982); P. Gardner, *The Lost Elementary Schools of Victorian England* (London, 1984); J.F.C. Harrison, *The Common People* (London, 1984); E. and S. Yeo, *Popular Culture and Class Conflict 1590–1914: Explorations in the History of Labour* (Brighton, 1981).

CHAPTER SIX

'Domestic Harmony, Public Virtue'

Catherine Hall

It used to be said that history was all about kings and queens. At school in the 1950s, we certainly learned more about the doings of mediaeval monarchs, the crowned heads of Europe and the great Victoria than about ordinary people, their work, their families, their dreams and desires. Ideas about history have changed since then and there is now far more attention paid to everyday lives. But the affairs of the royals, looked at anew through the lens of social history, can give fascinating insights into public attitudes to family, marriage and sexuality – key aspects of the nineteenth-century world.

Take the affair of Queen Caroline, the scandal that rocked the nation in 1820, seventeen years before Victoria came to the throne. In 1794 George, Prince of Wales, son of George III, had married Caroline of Brunswick. It was not a marriage for love, but for money. George was a pleasure-loving spendthrift, always on bad terms with his serious-minded and pious father on account of his extravagance, his dissolute habits, his sexual indiscretions (which included a secret marriage with a twice-widowed Roman Catholic) and his oppositional politics. In 1794, desperate for some financial aid, he agreed to marry the eminently suitable Caroline in return for the settlement of his debts. His father hoped that he would settle down, live a regular life and have children.

The union, however, was doomed from the start. George disliked Caroline for what he saw as her vulgar German ways, her talkativeness, her indiscretion. He was totally unprepared to change his way of life and the couple lived together only briefly. One child

6.1. Queen Caroline

was born, a princess, Charlotte, in 1796. Caroline was left living the restricted life of a royal bride but with no husband, trying to survive in a foreign country, a lonely and isolated figure.

George soon began to attempt to get rid of her. At his insistence a 'Delicate Investigation' was mounted in 1806 to establish whether Caroline had borne an illegitimate child, since that would give him grounds for divorce. No proof was forthcoming. Meanwhile, the whole world continued to know of the prince's amours. In 1814, Caroline agreed to depart from the country, leave her daughter and reside abroad in return for a regular income. She settled near Lake

Como and had little further connection with England.[1]

In 1820, George III died and the Prince of Wales succeeded his father. (He had held the position of Prince Regent for some time on account of his father's periodic bouts of insanity.) His first concern was to stop Caroline becoming queen. He announced that in churches throughout the kingdom her name should be excluded from the liturgy; no mention should be made of the existence of his wife. Caroline was furious and came hurrying back to England to claim her rightful place. She found immediate support amongst the radicals, who were glad of a stick with which to beat the king. Attempts at mediation failed. The king insisted on the introduction of a Bill of Pains and Penalties in the House of Lords, which if successful would have ended the marriage. Its purpose was to prove that Caroline was adulterous.

6.2. The trial of Queen Caroline, 1820

The public trial of the queen occupied the nation's imagination in the summer of 1820. Such a spectacle had never been seen before. For weeks the royal soap opera provided inches of column space in the national and provincial press as their lordships heard the evidence of scandal in high places, of illicit sexuality between mistress and servants, of marriage without love. The peers of the realm sat in judgement upon Caroline, the only woman in the chamber, contending with all the majesty of their lordships. Day after day, evidence was produced by a stream of witnesses of her mistakes, of her vulgarity, of her infidelities.

No television beamed into the nation's homes that summer but newspapers carried the story with all its salacious details from John O'Groats to Land's End, from burgeoning towns to tiny villages. The established national press now had its flourishing provincial counterparts. *Aris's Birmingham Gazette*, the *Manchester Mercury* or the *Leed Intelligencer*, for example, meant that Birmingham masters, Lancashire manufacturers and Yorkshire farmers, could have full knowledge of the trial within days. Better transport meant that pamphlets and broadsheets printed in London could soon be available in rural Essex or urban Liverpool. The new periodicals of the early nineteenth century carried reports and articles on the trial. Improved literacy made all this available to a growing reading public.[2] Meanwhile, songs were composed for the alehouse and clergymen fulminated on the state of England's morals from the pulpit. The nation awaited the outcome.

But public opinion, that new phenomenon of the eighteenth century, did not rally behind the king. Rather it swung behind the queen, victim of the king's power and might, a poor defenceless woman who needed protection. From the beginning the radicals had provided support for the queen, but this support broadened out, coming to include such diverse elements as bishops who could not support divorce, large sections of the middling ranks and the London crowd. Demonstrations, petitions, meetings and processions multiplied in London. Whenever Caroline appeared she could be sure of an escort, accompanying her to the House of Lords, ridiculing the hypocrisy of the monarchy, denouncing the king as the perpetrator of a double standard.

For the double standard was at the heart of the controversy. The king's philanderings had been well known for years, the subject of much malicious comment and caricature. What gave him the right to castigate the queen for infidelity, relying on the evidence of foreign informers for his case? Caroline became the symbol of persecuted womanhood, the victim of male aristocratic arrogance, the 'poor unprotected female'. The tales of the informers were disbelieved, the queen presented as 'wronged', a 'poor, fragile woman', a woman who had to be rescued from her fate by the true spirit of British justice. Decent men everywhere should rise to her defence and recover the good name of English manhood. 'I would blush for the British name – I would tremble for the fate of every woman in this country', trumpeted one commentator, 'if I did not see arrayed against this foul persecution, all the manly virtues of the land.'[3] The tenderness and respect with which women were treated in England, it was argued, were the great mark of superiority and civilisation. The king's action legitimated every ruffian abusing and insulting his wife, that wife whom he had promised to cherish and protect. It was the symbol of the degeneracy and decay of national morals. Men must rise up, reassert their 'manly virtues' and as fathers, husbands and brothers stand firm in a woman's cause. So powerful was the sense of chivalry that the London brassfounders and coppersmiths even mounted a full procession with steeds and armour in defence of the queen. The safest bulwark of the English crown, it was maintained, was its place in the popular heart. The brightest ornament of that crown should be its domestic virtue.

Meanwhile, women themselves were not slow to support Caroline. The ladies of Bath, Bristol, Exeter, Halifax, Leeds and Nottingham all presented their loyal addresses to the queen. Songsters appealed to the wives of Britain to resent the sufferings of Caroline:

> Attend ye virtuous British wives,
> Support your injured Queen,
> Assert her rights, they are your own
> As plainly may be seen.[4]

Faced with this groundswell of public opinion, George was forced to drop the case and the queen triumphed. A triumph that was, however, short-lived. Her place in the popular imagination faded rapidly. She was indeed a curious symbol of domestic virtue and it was domestic virtue that was being demanded of the monarchy. As John Bull, that legendary figure characterising the British way of life, carolled in his *Ode to George the Fourth and Caroline his wife*:

> A *Father* to the *nation* prove,
> A *Husband* to thy *Queen*,
> And safely in thy people's love
> Reign tranquil and serene.[5]

Kings, if they were to be popular, learnt George, must lead a proper domestic life. Fatherhood of the nation could not be achieved outside a decent marriage. This was a lesson well learnt by subsequent monarchs. Throughout the nineteenth century, Victoria was constantly represented as mother of her nation and of her children. More recently, the crisis surrounding the abdication in 1936 provided a potent demonstration of the continued importance of a respectable family life for the royals. The case of Queen Caroline had indeed marked a watershed.

Marriage and family life had long been at the heart of British culture. But the meaning of marriage and the organisation of family life did not remain fixed and unchanging. The economic, social and political transformation of Britain in the late eighteenth and early nineteenth centuries brought with it changes in the relations between men and women as well as the more frequently discussed changes in the relations between classes. The affair of Queen Caroline marked a moment at which some of those changes were registered in a public debate and one view of marriage was decisively rejected in favour of another. While the development of new industries and technologies, the growth of towns, the shifts in the nature of the state and the emergence of class society have all been well documented it is only relatively recently that historians have begun to pay attention to the ways in which family structures and individual women as well as men were placed in these processes. The demand for a domesticated monarch in 1820 only makes sense when considered in the context of changing views of marriage and family life. Those changing views were rooted in the dual revolutions: the industrial development that significantly affected Britain from the late eighteenth century and the impact of the French Revolution on British social and political life.

The supporters of Queen Caroline shared assumptions as to the proper forms of masculinity and femininity. They challenged the aristocratic code with its ideas of contract marriage and male sexual licence.[6] Instead they proposed a domesticated family life, marriage based on love and parental involvement with children (one of the criticisms of George was that he made Caroline leave her daughter). Such ideas had been part of the Puritan code of the seventeenth century.[7] But in the lax days after the Restoration Puritan morality was in decline. The late eighteenth century saw a powerful reworking of such concepts, particularly in the context of the religious revival which was taking place. The Evangelicals, an influential group which sought to purify the Anglican church from within and was led by such powerful figures as William Wilberforce, the hero of the anti-slavery movement, argued that Britain could only be saved from moral collapse and the danger of political revolution equivalent to that which had taken place in France by a fundamental reform of manners and morals. Such reform depended on the individual salvation of thousands of men and women. Through their individual conversions they would be inspired to lead lives guided by Christian morality. They would create religious households which collectively would provide a basis for a national social transformation.[8]

The best-known Evangelical writer was Hannah More, a woman from the margins of the landed gentry, who became a successful playwright and member of the London literary scene before her conversion to Evangelical Christianity in adulthood.[9] She gave up the theatre and the gay social world and devoted the rest of her life to the reform of manners and morals, whether by practical efforts such as the setting up of Sunday schools in her neighbourhood, or by wielding

6.3. Hannah More

the power of her pen. She wrote for all social classes. While her first books were designed to shame the aristocracy and gentry into improved patterns of behaviour she also turned her hand to easy-to-read moral tales for the labouring poor, especially after the French Revolution when the propertied of Britain worked hard to ensure that no such terror should disrupt their world. In 1809 she wrote a novel specifically to appeal to the middle class. Entitled *Coelebs in Search of a Wife*, it was a runaway success, going into many editions and selling many thousands of copies. *Coelebs* was the story of a virtuous young man's search for the perfect wife – the woman who would be a companion for himself, the mistress of his household, the mother of his children. The novel celebrated marriage and domesticity, it presented the home as the haven from the dangers of the world outside. It argued that men's place was in the public world of work and politics while women should properly confine themselves to the private world of family and children. Women, suggested More, occupy a smaller circle than men, but 'the perfection of a circle consists not in its dimensions, but in its correctness'.[10] It was natural for More that men and women should live their lives in 'separate spheres', as they came to be called, the public sphere of men, the private sphere of women.

Such ideas had a resonance far beyond the confines of Evangelical congregations. The Evangelicals worked tirelessly themselves to popularise their views, whether in the books and pamphlets which poured from their presses, in the parish work done by hundreds of Evangelical clergy and their thousands of energetic lay assistants, in the ceaseless philanthropic efforts which they inspired and organised or in the ways in which they carried their convictions into their households, their workplaces and their politics.[11]

The first generation of Evangelicals, led by William Wilberforce and Hannah More, were best known for their work in anti-slavery. This campaign was directly inspired by their religious beliefs, their conviction that all God's souls must be free. Their horror at the separation of slave mother and child and the refusal of a decent family life on the cotton and sugar plantations was also fuelled by their conviction of the central importance of a religious household. Evangelicals tended to be Tories and their campaigns on behalf of the slaves of other lands were branded as blatant hypocrisy by radicals in Britain who were subject to the repressive state policies fostered by Pitt and his colleague, Wilberforce, in the 1790s, and had to contend with Hannah More's stream of conservative polemic. But while their political conservatism was refused by many, their familial ideals found many echoes.

Evangelicals hoped to reform the working-class family through direct intervention. By the 1830s and 40s, the well-established voluntary routes such as encouraging working-class participation in Sunday schools where young boys and girls were not only taught to read the Bible but also learned their appropriate sex roles, were strengthened with forms of state legislation. The Children's Employment Commission, initially set up in 1840 to inquire into the work of children in the mines, had revealed shocking evidence as to the nature not only of child labour but also of women's work underground. This horrified the sensibilities of the middle-class male commissioners who were collecting the evidence and who, while quite content to employ female domestic servants in heavy labour in their homes, were unhappy about the kind of work they saw women doing in the mines. This inspired the campaign to end all female work underground. The Mines and Collieries Bill, including this clause, was spearheaded by Lord Ashley, the Evangelical Tory MP for Dorset, who believed that women's mission was to care for their families and that the moral fabric of society was threatened by their paid employment in the mines. Appealing to public humanity directly in the face of contemporary orthodoxies which stressed the importance of government not intervening in the economy, he succeeded, despite the strenuous opposition of the mine owners, in getting an Act through Parliament.[12]

But the success of new ideas about motherhood, home and family could not depend on the campaign zeal of any group, however determined and energetic. Domesticity had a powerful appeal to ordinary men and women across Britain. In a time of both rapid social and economic change and political turmoil the creation of a sense of order in home and personal life provided some security. By mid century, a somewhat secularised notion of separate spheres, which no longer had individual salvation at its heart, had become the common sense of the British nation, shared in different ways by most social groups.

That notion of separate spheres was rooted in the material changes which were taking place. In the eighteenth century, workplace and home were one and the same for artisans, tradesmen and merchants. Their workshops, shops and counting houses were under, next to, or behind their living quarters. The early nineteenth century saw the beginning of the separation between workplace and home.[13] This separation was partly inspired by the larger, purpose-built units of production such as the mill or the factory which were no longer so conveniently linked with living space. But sections of the middle class also increasingly desired, when finances permitted, to get away from the dense and dangerous town centres, rife with infection and the potential for political unrest, and create new homes, havens of peace

6.4. A warehouse in
Great Charles Street,
Birmingham

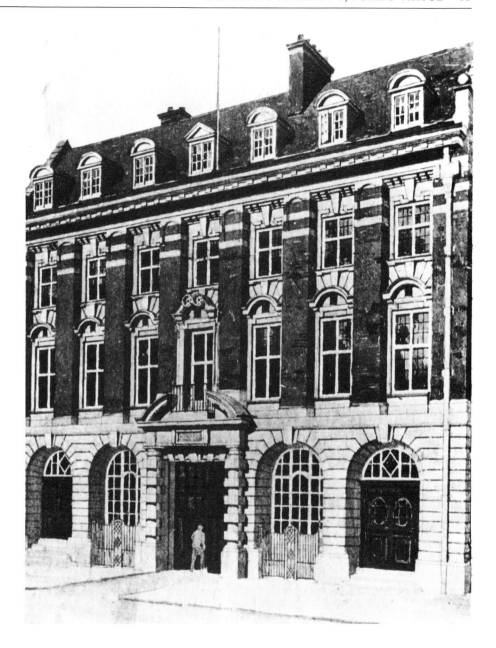

and quiet, set in suburban tranquillity. Such homes were to be characterised by comfort.

Patterns of work were also changing for the middle classes. Eighteenth-century traders and farmers, for example, expected all members of their families to contribute to the business which sustained their households. The wives of shopkeepers would help out in the shop, look after apprentices, check the orders when their husbands were away. Their sons and daughters would run errands and help in whatever ways they could from a very early age. Farmers' wives were busy in the dairy, kept ducks and hens, and managed a large household consisting of family and farm servants. But changes in the organisation of business together with new expectations as to the special role of women as wives and mothers were gradually resulting in the marginalisation of middle-class women from such a direct involvement in productive work.[14] Gentility for women was coming to be associated with being a dependant.

The story of James Luckcock, a Birmingham jeweller, illustrates many of these changes. A prodigious writer, Luckcock left an autobiography, poetry and some political and moral writings. Together with other sources these allow us to build some picture of his life. Born in 1761 into what he himself described as a 'humble sphere', he was apprenticed at 14 to a Birmingham plater. But by dint of hard work and application he became a manager in a large jewellery firm and eventually established his own business. A lifelong radical, he was involved in campaigns for freedom of speech, freedom of the press and the reform of the franchise.[15] His portrait now hangs in the corridors of Birmingham's Corporation building, a recognition of his contribution to the city's history. From his early manhood he was attached to a Unitarian congregation and was much influenced by its famous minister, the chemist and theologian Joseph Priestley, who was forced to leave the town in 1791 on account of his unpopular

6.5. James Luckcock

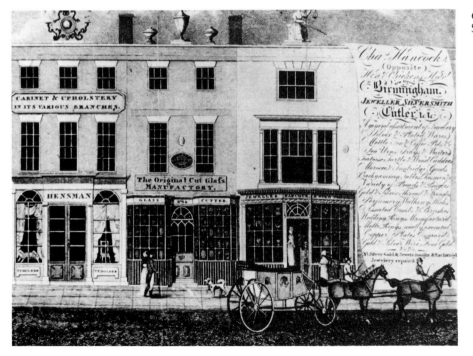

6.6. Hancock's Jewellery Shop, Birmingham

support for the French Revolution. Luckcock was active in organising the building of a new Sunday school for the Unitarians and he founded the Birmingham Brotherly Society, a society to help young apprentices to improve their education and prepare themselves for their responsibilities as masters, husbands and heads of households. Luckcock was a public man in all respects – moderately successful in his business, well known for his political and philanthropic activities.

Meanwhile he worked to create a domesticated private life and an existence for his wife in the private sphere of home and family. Having grown up in a world which assumed that women would work and contribute to their family's enterprise, he shared the growing disquiet among the middling ranks at the idea of their wives and daughters working for money. Such disquiet was linked with the notion of separate spheres and the assumption that it was a man's responsibility to provide for his dependants. When Luckcock first set up in business on his own he needed his wife's help – her labour as warehousewoman saved him vital cash. As soon as he could afford another hand, however, his wife stopped working in the warehouse and focused her energies on the home.[16]

6.7. A typical house in Hagley Road, Edgbaston

James Luckcock was one of the first to build a house in the salubrious new district of Edgbaston, designed for middle-class tenants, only three-quarters of a mile from the town centre but with something of the aura of country life. Edgbaston's landlord, the Evangelical Lord Calthorpe, stipulated in the leases that no workshops or manufactories should be established in the gardens or outhouses of his properties. Edgbaston was to be strictly residential, a new concept in middle-class housing.[17] Luckcock's first home, once he was in business independently, had been close to his workshop. In 1820 he was able to retire from business and make the move to Edgbaston. There he had constructed the home of his dreams, described for us in his little book *My House and Garden*. A modest semi-detached house, secluded from all the noises of the town, it had its own garden which he carefully planned and planted. The canal at the bottom of the garden was hidden with a hedge so that the rough boatmen would not be visible. Horse chestnuts, mountain ash and limes were laid out. Vases and pedestals with inscriptions, 'To Domestic Harmony', 'To Public Virtue' decorated the garden, together with figurines. Simple flowers were favoured, the 'humble cowslip' and 'unpretending foxglove'.[18] Here Luckcock delighted in his retirement, tending his garden, mixing with his neighbours and writing his autobiography with its detailed record of his commitment to domestic life. For Luckcock, like many men of his generation, such a life marked the epitome of his dreams. It was hard work and diligence which had made it possible but the cares and anxieties of business were gladly abandoned in favour of 'the sweet delights of home.'[19]

Those home comforts and delights were powerfully associated with the presence of a wife and children. But both the layout and furnishing of the home were significantly changing as well. The simple wooden benches and chairs of the eighteenth-century farm kitchen, where the whole household ate together, were augmented with a new parlour, a 'best' room, with wallpaper, carpets and curtains, pictures on the wall and a bellpull by the fireplace to call the maidservant who became an essential feature of the middle-class home.[20] In Edgbaston's villas there were special nurseries for the children, a dining-room replete with linen tablecloths, napkins, china and silverplated candelabra as well as drawing-rooms with handsome grates, comfortable covered sofas, books and bookcases, ornaments, musical instruments, tables for sewing and embroidery and family portraits.[21] Many of these items were products of the new industrial processes and, indeed, the foundation of many a middle-class fortune: the brass for the bellpull from Birmingham, the Staffordshire pottery or the Sheffield plate. In the bedrooms were chintz covers for the beds, light wallpapers and washstands which emphasised new standards of cleanliness. Such houses, however modest, had their own gardens and their privacy was protected with trees, hedges, gates, drives and walls.

These domestic values were not confined to the middle classes. Prominent among Queen Caroline's supporters were the well-known radicals William Cobbett and Samuel Bamford. Cobbett was a farmer and journalist, editor of the *Political Register* which was widely read by working people in the 1820s. He wrote a spirited defence of Queen Caroline. Bamford was a weaver, imprisoned for his part in the Peterloo massacre of 1819, when the yeomanry attacked an unarmed crowd. While in gaol he wrote two songs especially for the queen's cause.

Cobbett was an enthusiastic believer in domestic life. He was well aware of the changes which were affecting rural life and his celebrated *Rural Rides* documents the break-up of traditional patterns of agriculture and the increasing importance of wage labour. Cobbett deplored the collapse of the old system in which farm labourers had been a part of the farmer's household, eating at the farmhouse table and living in the farm.[22] Living-in servants had been part of the household of master and mistress, treated as dependants, supervised in their personal as well as their working lives, represented politically by their master. The decline of this living-in service and the parallel decline of apprenticeship in crafts and trades meant that young people, dependent on day labour, no longer had the buffer of an established household.[23] They had either to stay with their families or attempt to set up on their own. The paternalistic patterns of the past were deeply problematic but their collapse meant that labourers were potentially more vulnerable to the vagaries of the market. In this context, with punitive state policies on the Poor Law, it was family and kin who provided support. While Luckcock's home was a haven from the cares and anxieties of the businessman, the labouring poor, whether textile workers, agricultural labourers or miners, needed their homes as havens from heavy hours of labour, a boom and slump economy, and the fear of hunger. For Cobbett, as for Bamford, family could offset the miseries of the new industrial society. While the man had the responsibility to provide for his wife and children (though in reality the majority of working women needed paid employment for the family to survive economically), the woman would organise the household, manage what resources were available, and contribute to the family economy through her domestic skills. Such ideas, linked to the claim for a 'family wage', a wage that would ensure the man's ability to provide for his dependants, were becoming part and parcel of working-class culture in the early nineteenth century.[24]

The tale of Queen Caroline may seem a strange starting point for an investigation into family life in the early nineteenth century. But the royal family has come to symbolise the quintessentially British family, the family at the heart of the nation. The particular idea of family celebrated by Queen Caroline's supporters — where marriage was a partnership based on love, sexual fidelity was expected of both man and wife, and the home should provide a haven from the hostile world

– was a historically specific set of ideas that made sense in the changing conditions of the early nineteenth century. Those ideas became embedded in British social institutions, and indeed in the very houses we still inhabit.

Although this concept appealed powerfully to men and women across religion, class and politics, it had very different effects for the two sexes. Middle-class men were offered power, responsibility and opportunity in the public world but many middle-class women came to feel imprisoned and oppressed by the private sphere of the home and longed for economic and educational chances. Working-class men claimed a wage, a vote for themselves and the right to organise to defend their conditions of work. Meanwhile working-class women, forced into employment to survive, were criticised as unfeminine and their low pay was justified on the grounds that it was 'woman's work' and for 'pin money'. We are still living with some legacies of those ideas and that particular family form, though in many significant ways beliefs and patterns of behaviour have changed. The case of Queen Caroline reminds us that families, marriages, and patterns of sexual behaviour are not natural but social – that both private and emotional life have a history, a history which was central to the everyday life of our forebears.

Further reading

L. Davidoff and C. Hall, *Family Fortunes: Men and Women of the English middle class 1780–1850* (London, 1987); J. Gillis, *For Better, For Worse: British Marriages 1600 to the Present* (Oxford, 1986); A. John, *By the Sweat of their Brow. Women Workers at Victorian coal mines* (London, 1984); I. Pinchbeck, *Women workers and the Industrial Revolution 1750–1850* (London, 1981); J. Rendell, *The Origins of Modern Feminism: Women in Britain, France and the United States 1780–1860* (London, 1985); B. Taylor, *Eve and the New Jerusalem. Socialism and Feminism in the Nineteenth Century* (London, 1983); J. Weeks, *Sex, Politics and Society. The regulation of sexuality since 1800* (London, 1981).

CHAPTER SEVEN

The Victorian State: Order or Liberty?

V. A. C. Gatrell

Week by week nowadays law-and-order propagandists tell us that the threat of crime is a dominant problem of modern times. Crime is a social disease, we are told; it is increasing alarmingly, and it reflects the decay of our moral values, our self-discipline and our respect for authority. We have heard this so often that most of us are convinced that all of this must be so.

There is nothing new in this argument, however. Politicians, police chiefs and pundits of authoritarian inclination have been making political capital out of crime for the past 150 years. And they have been doing this even though crime has never seriously threatened the fabric of society, however offensive it might be to its individual victims. This applies even today. The cost of all reported thefts in England and Wales in 1980 was £551 million. This is less than the £800 million which in 1984 the controller of the Audit Commission for Local Authorities said could be saved if local councils were more prudent in their purchase of envelopes, refuse sacks, exercise books and tennis balls.

Why have these people kept telling us for so long that crime threatens our social order? Their message has always had concealed purposes behind it. Historically, one of these purposes has been quite transparent. By fanning public alarms about crime, and by ascribing to it a large moral, social and economic significance, they have justified the growth of the disciplinary state, which in modern times has become the main institutional source of authority and order. There have been few expressions of anxiety about crime in the past century and a half which have not predictably led to calls for more policemen and more efficient court procedures, stricter laws and extended bureaucratic control over the lives of the people. So useful is the fear of crime in this connection (one might well suspect) that if crime did not exist, those with an interest in extending state authority would have to invent it.

As a matter of fact, crime as a 'problem' was indeed first invented in the early nineteenth century. In the eighteenth century, 'crime' as a collective noun, denoting a measurable problem and symbolic of wider social indiscipline, had not yet been coined. The word still referred to the act of an individual. Eighteenth-century gentlemen referred to 'a crime', seldom if at all to 'crime'. This was partly because criminality seldom threatened their well-insulated lives. It was also because they were not as yet deeply worried about the pace of social change, and hence had no call to invest crime with the symbolic meanings it was soon to acquire.

7.1. Three prisoners at Derby Gaol

By the 1830s, by contrast, anxiety about change was widespread. Towns were expanding, pauperism was rising, more women and children were working, working people were increasingly politicised, and the threat of popular insurrection was never far from the minds of the elite. All of this invested crime with new significance. Crime became a vehicle on to which people could conveniently displace their anxieties about the future. It became an emblem of changes they deplored. That is why they began to *explain* it in terms of changes they deplored – like the growth of towns or changes in the family. It was easier to say that crime was caused by these things, and by the immorality and indiscipline of the underclasses, than to acknowledge that it might be caused by inequalities of income and opportunity. Crime has never lost these displaced meanings which it first acquired in the early nineteenth century. Probably now it never will.[1]

The raw material which gave rise to the invention of 'crime' as an aggregated social problem was the publication from 1805 onwards of annual data on prosecutions. These prosecution rates increased dramatically up to the late 1840s. We know now that this was not necessarily because crime increased: it would be difficult to prove that it did any such thing. The rates increased for reasons that had little to do with the real incidence of crime at all. More hitherto tolerated forms of behaviour were being criminalised, the propertied classes were becoming more anxious about crime, prosecution was becoming cheaper and easier and policing more effective.[2]

But of course when they analysed prosecution figures, early Victorians were no more critical of their meaning than many of us are today. From that day to this, questionable crime rates have always been used to inflame unreal fears, and to give shape to imagined problems. 'Crime in England has increased 700 per cent', one typical apologist fumed in *Blackwood's Magazine* in 1844: 'in Ireland about 800 per cent, and in Scotland above 3,500 per cent. What', he asked, 'is . . . to be the fate of a country in which the progress of wickedness is so much faster than the increase in population?' His explanation for this imagined state of affairs also sounds a familiar note to modern ears. He spoke with distaste of the increasing anonymity of urban life and the corrupting effects of affluence on working people and the young. He deplored 'habits of idleness and insubordination' among the common people. And (inevitably) he worried about the decay of the family: the factory employment of women destroyed the familial bond and 'emancipated the young from parental control'.[3] What he was really worried about, clearly, was not so much crime as social change, and the threats social change was delivering to his own security. Early Victorian texts of this kind pioneer a mode of argument which has shaped images of crime ever since. Modernise the phraseology a little, and it might be Mr Norman Tebbit talking.

The effects of this way of thinking on British history were profound. For 150 years, as implied above, the main beneficiary of anxieties about crime has been the disciplinary state. And again, we are confronted here with something quite 'modern'. In the eighteenth century the state kept a low profile in law-enforcement. Law was enforced by local elites, unpaid JPs and locally appointed parish constables. Punishment could be draconian but not many were prosecuted; very few were hanged. Most sanctions which kept people in their place were exerted not bureaucratically but face-to-face and informally, by employer on workman, landlord on tenant, neighbour on neighbour. Gentlemen were content with this system, not only because it worked and was cheap, but also because they feared the state more than they feared the populace. Social order was quite secure. It could be taken for granted. Like their forefathers a century before (especially if they were Whigs), they thought their main political obligation was not the defence of order, but rather the defence of their own liberties and privileges against the ambitions of central despotism. English liberty, not law-and-order, was the catch-phrase of the eighteenth century.[4]

By the 1830s, needless to say, the security of the social order could no longer be taken for granted. The state now began to look like the only plausible bulwark between order and anarchy, between property and the plebeian mass. In the interests of *order* (people were beginning to say), a little liberty might have to be sacrificed. Edwin Chadwick, for example, pleaded for a centralised police system in these terms in 1839. You cannot, he argued, enjoy liberty if you do not enjoy order first.[5] This kind of argument has justified the expansion of the disciplinary state ever since. Libertarian opinion has never been silenced in Britain. Nonetheless, the primary value around which most social debate and policy was henceforth to be organised came to be 'order', not 'liberty'.

The state began accordingly to assume an increasing control of law-enforcement in ways eighteenth-century gentlemen would have deplored. The most familiar bench-mark in this process occurred in 1829, when Peel scared Parliament (not least by the selective quotation of 'crime' rates) into sanctioning the introduction of full-time professionalised policing in London. Designed to be impersonal agents of the law and of central policy, police on the metropolitan model were extended to boroughs and counties in and after the 1830s, and made mandatory throughout the country in 1856.[6]

Central control of policing was always camouflaged by the powers of appointment and finance left to local watch committees and the

7.2. A City of London policeman

like. Even so, from the mid nineteenth century onwards Whitehall increasingly called the tune to which policemen had to dance. For example, central inspection was introduced in 1856; from the 1870s the Home Office regulated pay and discipline across the country; while after 1890 mutual aid agreements between forces facilitated the exchange of constables to help other forces confronted by industrial unrest.

7.3. Cheshire police on duty in Yorkshire during the 1893 miners' strike

Most interestingly, Scotland Yard came to play an important part in the centralising process, too. Because London was the national and imperial capital, the Home Office had directly controlled metropolitan policing from 1829 onwards. It turned this agency to powerful effect. Under Home Office direction, most new police policies and practices were first evolved and tested in London. Scotland Yard thus set the pace for an increasing specialisation and centralisation of police functions which Peel could never have foreseen. All provincial police forces were gradually affected by it.

Detectives offer one example. In Peel's day, plainclothes spy systems of any kind had been held in deepest suspicion. When the Home Office established a rudimentary detective force in 1842, it had done so rather surreptitiously. By the 1870s, however, this little body smelt of corruption, and the stink exploded in 1877. What was for that date the longest ever trial at the Old Bailey resulted in the conviction of Inspector Meiklejohn and Chief Inspectors Druscovitch and Palmer for obstructing investigation into a major turf fraud. The Home Office seized the opportunity to overhaul the detective system, and to public acclaim a much augmented CID was established in 1878. The number of criminal arrests by detectives in London rose from 13,128 in 1879 to 18,343 in 1884. The status and continuing expansion of the CID – and of detective work throughout the country – was henceforth assured.

7.4. Manchester detectives, 1890

No less significantly, secondly, it was the Home Office and Scotland Yard which in 1869 established the criminal records system whose computerised descendant many worry about today. In its early years the system was primitive enough, to be sure, and its procedures look quaint today. It quickly became unwieldy as the names of convicted criminals in its registers multiplied unmanageably. But it got better. Photography (and after 1902 fingerprinting) soon transformed the system, and even the regular circulation of simple information sheets to provincial forces brought satisfying results. By 1880 the director of the CID was convinced that the British police had no more efficient weapon against the criminal than its central records. The more covert surveillance of 'enemies within', incidentally, was being regularised at the same time with the formation of the Special Branch in 1884 to keep tabs on Irish Fenian bomb-planters.[7]

In view of these and similar developments, it is not surprising that the cost of policing in England and Wales rose from £1.5 million in 1861 to £5 million in 1901 (faster, by the way, than the population and the cost of reported crime). Police numbers more than doubled from 20,750 to 44,593: the metropolitan force nearly tripled in size.[8]

We should remember, too, that the Victorian state was also assuming increasing control of prisons and of the ancient discretionary areas of sentencing and prosecution. It extended paid magistrates' jurisdiction over lesser felonies to bypass jury trial and speed the processing of offenders. At the same time, more and more statutes and by-laws extended police control over a bewildering array of social groups, from vagrants to pawnbrokers, from habitual criminals to feckless parents, from pornographers to drunks. The result was that by 1900 what policemen, magistrates, prison governors and even judges had to do across the country was being largely dictated from Whitehall. The criminal department of the Home Office grew correspondingly. Set up in 1870, by the 1880s it had become the most important department in the Home Office. By 1906, it was dealing with a third of all Home Office business.[9] The policeman-state which today we take for granted had come of age. Its continuing expansion in the twentieth century was now inevitable.

The impact of these developments in taming the later Victorian poor was substantial. Crime rates declined steadily for about half a century after the 1850s, arguably because Britain's street criminals were unable to evade the controls to which they were increasingly subjected. They were sitting targets. And we may be sure, too, that the coercive policeman-state was far more of a presence in working-class life than the more benign state which our history textbooks approvingly emphasise (which began to take an interest in factories, sanitation or education, for example). We can measure this through the accelerating impact of law-enforcement on the poor, against whom it was mainly directed. In 1805 a mere 3267 males in England and Wales were tried by jury for indictable offences. By the 1840s the numbers had risen to 25,000 or so, and very many more were being dealt with summarily in magistrates' courts. By 1901, if you were male (regardless of age, class and habitat), you had an astonishing 1 in 24 chance of being arrested or summoned for an indictable or non-indictable offence in that year alone. If you lived in a city, and were visibly poor, unemployed and young, your chances of a coercive experience of the law were several times higher. Across several years you were *certain* to have cause to resent a policeman's intervention in your life. The poor protested as best they could. By the 1900s the metropolitan police commissioner was complaining that 20 per cent of all metropolitan constables were being injured annually by their resentful targets.[10]

The assumption that a strong disciplinary state was the only defence against criminal anarchy in a mass society was not the only reason for the growth of the state. But we can see now why it was among the most important. Even by the 1860s the jurist J.F. Stephen identified the state primarily in its role as law-enforcer. He implied that this was how the populace experienced the state as well: 'The administration of criminal justice is the commonest, the most striking, and the most interesting shape, in which the sovereign power of the state manifests itself to the great bulk of its subjects.'[11] By the 1870s the conservative MP J.H. Scourfield, was more emphatic: 'If anybody were called on to portray the advancing civilization of England, it might be fitly conveyed by the representation of a prison.' The *Pall Mall Gazette* complained of the threat to 'individual liberty' from the prevailing compulsion 'to drill, discipline and dragoon us all into virtue'. And the feminist Josephine Butler announced that 'police government in its worst forms combines the evil of extreme centralisation with the activity, in every corner of the nation, of a vast and numerous agency of surveillance'.[12]

These were not extremist or isolated voices. From the 1880s many recognised that in pursuit of order, the British had unwittingly sanctioned the growth of a new form of social power. This was the power of state bureaucracy. Once set up, bureaucracy was capable of taking on a life of its own, of generating its own momentum. 'Every great public department', one jurist noted, had become 'a centre of force and influence which may rival all the more desultory forces of public opinion.' The historian Ramsay Muir observed in 1910 that 'if all the legislation of the last half-century by which the daily routine of English life has been affected could be traced to its source, it would

7.5. Bristol police
performing cutlass drill

certainly be found that a very large proportion of this legislation is
essentially bureaucratic in origins'; bureaucracy thereby fuelled its
own expansion.[13]

You do not need a conspiratorial view of ruling-class motives to
explain the expansion of this machinery. The appetite for control was
enlarged by what it fed upon. Law-and-order campaigns from the mid
nineteenth century onwards have been largely orchestrated not merely
by the politicians who shape (and occasionally follow) public opinion,
but also by the panoply of experts who are both a product of state-
formation and its ongoing cause: Home Office officials, police
commissioners, prison doctors and governors, and the like.

People of this kind repeatedly assessed the shortcomings of the
systems they operated in terms of their efficiency and rationality.
When expedient, they exaggerated the threat of crime to justify the
bureaucracy's further expansion and specialisation. (This is not to
deny that they often believed their own arguments.) They themselves

generated data (like statistics on crime and recidivism) to prove there were still problems to respond to. Through enquiry into, and ever-sharper categorisation of deviant areas, they brought problems into view to which earlier generations had been healthily indifferent. Thus piecemeal, and without long-term premeditation, they endlessly renewed their case for the continuing expansion of their own personnel, statutory powers and obligations. They found ready collaborators in Parliament and government, an uncritical press, and a respectable public whose anxieties they constantly refuelled. In this quite literal sense the Victorian state, like our own, began to shape, inflate, even to invent, the criminal problems which its purpose was to eradicate.

Take one example among many: the invention of the problem of 'professional' crime in the later nineteenth century.[14] In sober fact, Victorian crime was remarkably unprofessionalised. Most thefts were petty and opportunistic. Even when habitual, they were born of deprivation, and the loot was inconsiderable. It is true that gangs of organised thieves haunt the pages of blue-books, social surveys, and even novels from Dickens' time onwards, and protection rackets always flourished in London's East End. There was nothing new about these, however: the canting jargon of pickpockets and swellmobsmen can be traced back to Elizabethan times. If anything, by the later nineteenth century this tradition was declining. Compulsory schooling was cutting off its sources of recruitment; police supervision was making it difficult for gangs to re-form. Indeed the policeman-state was proving a huge success. 'Order' was being maintained even if 'liberty' was not. The rates for nearly all indictable crimes were actually declining after about 1860. They continued to do so until 1914.

Meanwhile, at the Old Bailey at the end of the century, trials for the 'professional' crime of burglary refuse to reveal booty much more spectacular than boots, clothes, food, and occasional silver candlesticks and spoons. Middlesex Quarter Session records refuse to expose many who were more 'professional' than (say) William Condon, four times convicted for stealing respectively a watch, a manicure set, clothing and a bicycle. Towards the end of his career, in 1910, he was convicted for breaking and entering to steal jewellery and clothing worth some £90. Men like this were nuisances, and on their victims' behalf they were worth catching and punishing. They were not, however, a threat to society. And the national economy could easily afford them, too. Reported burglary in 1899 cost Londoners £88,406, or a trivial 3d. per head. The metropolitan police cost twelve times as much.

7.6. The Portsmouth
police force, 1865

This cheerful outlook, however, was no impediment to the ongoing disciplinary enterprise. If a criminal problem did not exist the state and its henchmen would have to find one. They proceeded to do so. Crime rates, as usual, provided the excuse for one of the more prolonged and artificial moral panics in British criminal history. While in the later nineteenth century the rates for larceny, homicide, wounding and assaults were declining, burglary rates remained stable. The hunt was plausibly on for the professional burglar, creature of fantasy though he might be. In the 1880s the press began to peddle bloodcurdling images of a London at the mercy of criminals with low foreheads and beetling brows and eyes that were suspiciously close together.

There had been panics about such people before. The most famous had occurred after two released convicts had garrotted (or mugged) the MP Hugh Pilkington on Pall Mall in 1862.[15] This new panic was similarly set in motion by a small spate of armed burglaries in London between 1877 and 1886. The Home Office fed newspapers and Parliament with alarming figures on this phenomenon. It allowed metropolitan constables to be issued if need be with revolvers (one more characteristically *ad hoc* but never-to-be-retracted addition to the armoury of the state). Parliament debated flogging armed criminals, and in its inimitable way, *The Times* chipped in. Had they read that organ, William Condon and his like would have been surprised to learn that the burglar nowadays:

is fully equipped for battle, and carries arms of precision. . . . He sets out on his raids with the deliberate intention of killing and maiming. . . . Violence, if not actual murder, is all in the night's work. . . . There seems no good reason, the protest of mealy-mouthed philanthropists notwithstanding, why society should not avail itself of the obvious means of protection against its pitiless foe.[16]

Behind all this the influence of the Home Office was vital. The Home Office statistician Edward Troupp drew on the increasingly sophisticated records system at Scotland Yard to expose the alarming scale of recidivism. The 1895 Committee on Prisons duly announced that recidivism was not only the most important criminal question of the age, but worse, 'a growing stain on our civilisation'. Habitual criminals and hard-core professionals (the most recidivist of all), it said, should be subjected to sentences of preventive detention of indeterminate length.[17] In Sir Robert Anderson, ex-head of the CID, the Home Office found a public spokesman for this view who could plausibly call himself an expert. Anderson reminded those 'humanity-mongerers' who thought indeterminate sentences a bit much (not quite in the spirit of English liberty) that 'the extermination of the unfit is one of the plainest of natural laws'. After all, he added (in a mode which the twentieth century was to make ever more familiar), 'never a night passes that some crime of this kind is not committed in the metropolis. No one can be certain, as he shuts his door and lies down to sleep, that the sanctity of his home will not be thus outraged before morning.'[18]

The outcome of this long campaign was one of the most extraordinary Acts in British penal history, the 1908 Prevention of Crime Act. This had its benign face: it introduced borstals for young offenders in place of prison. And admittedly its sentence of preventive detention for the three times convicted felon who led 'a persistently dishonest life' was limited to a ten-year maximum: Anderson did not get the indeterminate sentence he and the Home Office had hoped for. Nonetheless the preventive detention was to be served in addition to and after a sentence of penal servitude, and it introduced a new principle in British penology. It sanctioned a punishment not for a crime actually committed, but for one which might be committed in future. It punished a man 'not for doing what he did, but for being what he was'.

The Act proved to be an absurdity. The hard-core professional turned out to be a figment of the bureaucratic imagination. In its first seven months, 112 men and one woman were sentenced under the Act. Although all were habitual thieves none was recognisably professional. Most differed little from the deprived petty larcenists who took up most court time. One had stolen a pair of boots, another a shilling, another four dishes. When Winston Churchill became Home Secretary in 1910, he was so shocked by this that he threatened to repeal the Act unless it was confined to those who were 'a real danger to society'. The trouble was that juries could find no such people: the numbers of those committed under the Act slumped dramatically. Reviewing the Act in 1932, an official committee found that most of its victims had been 'men with little mental capacity ... whose frequent convictions testify as much to their clumsiness as to their persistence in crime.' The Act had been introduced on the flimsiest of justifications, in response to an invented problem. But that has often been precisely how the state has expanded its powers. It stayed on the statute book until 1948 notwithstanding.[19]

Moral panics of the kind that led to the Prevention of Crime Act always look foolish in retrospect. Future historians will surely contemplate those of our own age with just as jaundiced an eye. And since panics are two-a-penny nowadays, they will have much to write about. Our moral police have become very good at organising and exploiting public anxieties about social order, moral values and 'discipline' (television helps them, of course). And with good reason too. Unreal though they usually are, such panics are always useful to them. They not only legitimise the authority of the state. They invariably provide opportunities to extend it as well. There is now no reason in logic or history to believe that the policeman-state will not expand infinitely in future. The Victorians were not quite as systematic as we are in the art of justifying this growth. We tread in their footsteps nonetheless.

Further reading

V. Bailey (ed.), *Policing and Punishment in Nineteenth-century Britain* (London, 1981); C. Emsley, *Policing and its Context, 1750–1870* (London, 1983); V.A.C. Gatrell, B. Lenman and G. Parker (eds), *Crime and the Law: the Social History of Crime in Western Europe since 1500* (London, 1980); D. Jones, *Crime, Protest, Community and Police in nineteenth-century Britain* (London, 1982); D. Philips, *Crime and Authority in Victorian England: the Black Country, 1835–1860* (London, 1977).

CHAPTER EIGHT

A Union without Unity

Roy Foster

'You may trace Ireland through the statute-book of England as a wounded man in a crowd is tracked by his blood.'[1] Thomas Moore, the Irish romantic poet, made that remark in 1824, and it remains a vivid image. But Irish history in the late eighteenth and early nineteenth centuries is about *more* than the relationship of Ireland to England – important though it is.

The period certainly includes a series of attempts to resolve the constitutional relations between Ireland and England: it begins with one, in 1782, and ends with the beginning of another, in 1870. In between, Ireland presented a constant problem for British administrations trying to fit it into the Victorian state. But over and over again, what is most striking is the different and incomprehensible nature of what went on in Ireland; and the contradictions between Irish reality and English perceptions.

In the late eighteenth century, Ireland was an important part of the British Empire, integrated into the framework of imperial commerce and politics. The scale of Dublin, laid out with tremendous ambition and style, always amazed travellers.[2] But it also made them rather uneasy, because the rest of the country seemed so spectacularly poor. The Irish commercial and agricultural economy was capable of producing considerable wealth, but the poverty in parts of the country was astounding.

The picture is a varied one. Ireland was not just a backward agricultural economy, despite the impression of mud cabins and pigs given by so many travellers. There were thriving local centres of agricultural industry, and a lively commercial culture. The Irish agrarian economy in the late eighteenth century responded very profitably to the early English industrial revolution; sophisticated transport systems, and a developing market economy, were creating wealth and a middle class.[3]

This should be remembered along with the traditional picture of a Georgian aristocracy ruling over an oppressed peasantry. There was a minority Protestant elite which excluded the Catholic majority from civil and political rights: the 'Ascendancy' world. But there was also an urban Catholic middle class in the making, gaining influence in unobtrusive ways, and running the economies of prosperous cities like Cork.

Their commercial power was partly a result of the fact that their formal ownership of land was so restricted; though Catholics were about three-quarters of the population they owned only 5 per cent of the land (although they could hold it on leases, sometimes very profitably). Inequalities were striking, and reflected passionate memories of seventeenth-century power struggles. But any realistic view of Ireland in the late eighteenth century has to emphasise vitality at least as much as stagnation.

Moreover, around 1780 the results of imperial and political crisis in Britain had begun to affect Ireland. The American Revolution not only began an ideological ferment; it also (more potently) aroused commercial resentment at Ireland's exclusion from colonial trade in the 1770s. A native gentry 'Volunteering' movement, organised rather like contemporary reform agitations in Britain, brought extra-parliamentary pressure to bear on the issue of Ireland's access to a free import and export trade. And the parliament at Dublin – essentially a limited assembly, carefully managed by the British government – began to agitate for a greater degree of legislative independence.

This was granted in 1782, though largely as a result of political crisis in England.[4] A so-called 'constitutional revolution' produced concessions which gave this colonial (and Protestant) assembly a more autonomous status, claimed by 'Patriot' politicians like Henry Grattan. But there are contradictions here too: the constitutional readjustment was mostly rhetorical. Any further steps that the parliamentary opposition took towards political 'reform' had to be very cautious because that at once raised the spectre of admitting the Catholic majority to full political rights, which threatened to upset the system of Protestant 'Ascendancy' established from the Glorious Revolution.

Grattan's parliament was determined to stay exclusive. Though Catholic disabilities were relieved by a series of Acts (including one giving them the vote, which was more than Catholics had in England), such amelioration invariably came about through pressure from the British government. Native 'Patriotism' was a very limited growth.

The Irish Protestant gentry class saw themselves as Irishmen with English civil rights; sharing an English king, but entitled to their own government. Meanwhile, they continued to be manipulated by the traditional arts of English influence and patronage until manipulated out of existence by the Act of Union in 1800.

The limitations and contradictions of 'colonial nationalism' were obvious to those contemporaries excluded from the Ascendancy world. And these were not just Catholics; there was another out-group, the Protestant Dissenters in religion – notably the Presbyterians of Ulster. Belfast was the one city in Ireland to share in the British industrial revolution. It was also the centre of a thriving, avant-garde political culture, much influenced by contemporary radicalism, especially (after 1789) the French variety. From this date, their ideology of libertarian politics, derived from John Locke and reinforced by the American revolution, took a new turn.

It was from Belfast that a radical political society – the United Irishmen – evolved in the early 1790s, theoretically committed to an independent Irish Republic, on a pluralist basis, for Catholic and Protestant. In fact, most of the United Irishmen were not particularly enamoured of Catholics, and expected radical evolution to educate them out of religious bigotry. But as it happened, events in Ireland would take the opposite trend, and educate many of the radicals into sectarian attitudes instead.

The most influential United Irishman, Wolfe Tone, forged the vital link between the society and France: as Britain became embroiled in war with revolutionary France, francophile Irish radicals were suppressed and went underground.[5] The Irish situation in the 1790s became part of the world of international espionage and destabilis-ation tactics; the radical-chic culture of Belfast and Dublin had to become serious business. In 1796, an unsuccessful French invasion force arrived off the south-west coast – large enough to wreak havoc if it could have landed.[6]

Political frustration, French negotiations and ruthless suppression by the wartime government laid the fuse which exploded in the Rebellion or Rising of 1798: not an egalitarian revolution on the French model, but a bloody peasant uprising with sectarian overtones. Catholic rebels were put down with horrific force by the local Protestant yeomanry. It reflected the increasing sectarian tension in Irish rural life, noticeable from the 1790s and demonstrated in the formation of ultra-Protestant Orange Lodges as well as Catholic secret societies dedicated to rooting out Protestantism. This in turn reflected not only events in Irish politics but also a more fundamental tension over land occupation in densely populated rural Ireland, especially after restrictions had been lifted on Catholics owning land.

The never-never land of 'colonial nationalism' was over. The Pitt government brought in an Act of Union in 1800 which abolished the Irish parliament and reformed the electoral system, sending 100 Irish

8.1. The murder of a drummer boy by rebels in 1798

MPs to Westminster instead. The theory was to integrate Ireland and England, politically and administratively. It was also supposed to integrate Catholics into the political nation, allowing them into parliament on a safely diluted basis. But the idea of a modernising, integrating, liberalising and emancipating measure failed. Political opposition was too strong to allow emancipation of Catholics, and the rest of the theory was doomed too.

This was not because of the irrepressible nature of Irish 'national-ism' – still at a very tentative stage of development. It had more to do with economics. The prosperity brought to the Irish economy by the French wars collapsed after Waterloo; the ensuing crisis was blamed on the Union. But the basis of the Irish economy had been unsound since the 1790s, and Britain had entered the stage of industrialisation where Ireland simply could not compete. It could not be accommodated comfortably in Pitt's master-plan, economically or politically. Integration simply would not work.

This would be the lesson of the Union. By 1800 Irish society had developed several complex strains, existing in an unmodernised and only patchily industrialised country. There was the colonial-nationalist gentry culture; the special traditions of Ulster, distinctively industrial-ised and distinctively Protestant; the bourgeois commercial Catholic culture, prepared to demand its civil rights; and the continuing Catholic peasant culture in the country at large, representing the great majority of a rapidly escalating population.

This complex, evolving society was very difficult for outsiders to understand; hence the reliance of English opinion on stereotypes of Irish life which stressed poverty and backwardness. In fact, the varied and localised Irish economy continued to expand in several sectors during the early nineteenth century, though competition from Britain killed off many of the growing industries. In many areas a prosperous farming class had evolved. The other constant stereotype was violence: at a time when England was becoming a 'peaceable kingdom', the Irish were supposedly resorting to faction fights, rural terrorism and breaking heads. This perception did reflect a powerful tradition in rural Ireland of 'alternative' structures of intimidation and enforcement, exercised through peasant secret societies which adopted a bewildering number of names.[7] This was the tradition which had taken over in 1798; it continued throughout the nineteenth century as an attempt to enforce, or retain, what was popularly perceived as a right order of rural relationships.

There was very little 'nationalism' or even 'politics' in this; the issues were usually local, anti-Protestant and directed towards land occupation. Dislocations in the rural economy and the inexorable pressure of population (which doubled over the eighteenth century, and had reached 8 million by the 1840s): these were the underlying conditions. But to English perceptions, it simply demonstrated that the Irish were not yet civilised. This went with the third stereotype: the Irish were not only poor and violent, they were Catholic. And this was interpreted as meaning priest-ridden, superstitious and disloyal. The Catholic cause, campaigning for political representation, would be the potent mobilising factor which brought the Irish crisis home to English politics.

But there were elements in Ireland that were neither poor nor violent, and often were not Catholic either. There was Ulster, largely Protestant since the seventeenth century, with an economy diversified and industrialised enough to respond energetically to post-war conditions, and where prosperity became closely associated, in the Ulster mind, with the Union. Elsewhere in Ireland too there were many middle-class people oriented towards London as their capital, the empire as their birthright, and Westminster as their Parliament. By the mid nineteenth century you did not have to be from Ulster, or a landlord, to share these identifications; the character of Phineas Finn, created by Trollope as the quintessential young Irishman on the make in London, is neither.[8] It is this tradition that sought a political voice for Ireland within the British system, and looked for a devolved status within the empire as the best way of reconciling the Irish difference with the inevitable closeness of Britain. At the end of the period, in 1870, it was just about to express itself in the demand for 'Home Rule'. But first we have to see how the other Irish traditions imposed themselves on English politics.

The early nineteenth century saw the issue of Catholic Emancipation detonate a crisis in Irish politics, and begin a constitutional revolution in Britain. In Ireland, the masses were mobilised politically in Daniel O'Connell's Catholic Association. And here was a vital fact for the future of Irish politics: a sophisticated mass organisation, based on subscriptions, officials, co-ordinated local campaigns and close integration with the Catholic Church, happened *before* the industrialisation and modernisation of much of the country.[9] This precocious development meant that Irish politics, and Irish party identifications, would remain locked into confessional forms and would be implicitly sectarian rather than class-based.

Daniel O'Connell himself epitomises this: this scion of old Gaelic gentry family in Kerry, speaking Irish as his first language, a great popular lawyer, a hero preserved in Irish folklore. But he is also a European figure, educated in France, who invented the language of Catholic liberalism in politics; a radical, integrated into the English political system, a passionate voice against the slave trade and the Corn Laws, an avid reader of Bentham and Godwin; and he believed deeply in the necessity to modernise Ireland.

Again, English observers missed these paradoxes; they saw only the organisation of the Irish peasantry into a subversive movement which threatened to overturn the entire political system. Certainly, O'Connell forced Catholic Emancipation on to the political agenda by a series of audacious challenges.[10] Then he began to agitate for repeal of the Act of Union, using similar tactics. But he was not a separatist like Tone – he is really closer to the Phineas Finn tradition. He often hinted that he would settle for a subordinate parliament; he declared effusive allegiance to the unreceptive figure of Queen Victoria; he worked closely with the Whigs in government and in opposition. And his tactics were essentially pacific; he constantly emphasised that no attempt at Irish separatism was worth shedding blood, and that the means of achieving so-called freedom would affect the kind of freedom achieved.

It was this approach that alienated the radical wing of the Repeal movement – the Young Ireland group, deeply affected by German romanticism and the cult of 'the Nation' (which was the name of their very influential newspaper). They appealed romantically (and safely) to dead 'patriots', like the men of 1798, who were now co-opted into a sacred tradition of national liberation, which they had been very far from representing at the time.

Young Ireland mounted a sort of cultural offensive, in which the writing of versions of Irish history became a political weapon, and a synthetic ballad literature delivered endless exhortations about the soul of the nation and the vital importance of the Irish language

8.2. Daniel O'Connell's
house, Derymane,
County Kerry

8.3. O'Connell
addressing a meeting at
Trim

(though few Young Irelanders spoke it).[11] By the early 1840s, the various strains of Irish identity had found their different voices. The Protestant 'Ascendancy' were fully integrated into Union and empire: the gentry through service in the army and the colonies, the urban Protestant petit-bourgeoisie through Orangeism and political activity on the unreformed town corporations. The Belfast business classes and their dependants had prospered through an industrial economy which they saw as dependent on political Unionism. Some Protestant intellectuals were trying to reconcile the demands of their religious-cultural identity with the idea of Irishness.[12] And the Catholic nation, politically mobilised by O'Connell, had come to see its identity as vaguely separate. Never ready to define what 'Repeal' actually meant, they identified it with economic betterment and a Catholic millennium. But a more specific sense of separation was nurtured by the Romantic nationalism of Young Ireland.

The response of the Victorian state was to treat Ireland, incomprehensible as ever, as a special case; even as a laboratory for administrative experiment. When Sir Robert Peel came into conflict with O'Connell, his strategy was to counter with drastic administrative reform – in which he was following a long-established tradition.[13] In the 1830s and 1840s, the British state in Ireland took initiatives which they could never have introduced in England. They imposed a centralised, state-funded system of non-religious elementary education. They created a centralised, professional police force.[14] They clipped the wings of the Protestant Established Church. They endowed a Catholic seminary at Maynooth.[15] They tried to reorganise Irish university education. They set up centrally-funded fever hospitals and lunatic asylums. The mechanisms of Irish government made radical administrative initiatives possible (though there were still glaring anomalies in areas like local government). But there was one area where interference had to go very gingerly; private property. In Ireland this inevitably meant land.

By the 1840s, government investigations into this fundamental question had run into thousands of pages. The land problem tended to be interpreted as a question of occupation: too many tenants, on an insecure basis, unprepared to make economic returns under a parasitic and under-investing landlord system. The usual answer was to increase the size of the holdings and reduce the number of tenants, providing security of tenure and creating a rural labourer force to approximate more closely to farming on the English model. Nowadays, the problem is perceived more in terms of structural and production difficulties arising from imbalances built into the Irish agrarian economy, exacerbated by the phenomenal growth of population.[16] But what was stressed by investigations like the Devon

Commission was the inability and lack of will of the tenants and the failure of social authority on the part of the landlords.

Intense subdivision, tiny holdings and a necessary dependence on the potato diet were the obvious results. Inexorable population pressure, probably based on early and fertile marriages enabled by the potato economy,[17] had created sustained growth and an accompanying pressure on living standards. This condemned large sectors of the population, especially in the west and south-west, to an insecure dependence on one crop.

The picture was a varied one; elsewhere in the island the agricultural economy was diversified and productive, greatly increasing both tillage and grazing output in the early nineteenth century. But by about 1840 it was clear that Ireland, which had seemed quite dynamic in 1780, had failed (outside Belfast) to participate in the kind of industrialisation which could sustain its population. The growth rate was beginning to slow down; marriages were taking place later; emigration was soaring.[18] Finally in 1845 the unthinkable happened; the potato crop failed nationally.

Previous local famines had created severe distress, but the horrors of 1845–9 beggar description. In the areas dependent upon the potato, roads and ditches were crowded with figures described again and again as walking skeletons, dying of disease as well as starvation. The fact that severe distress tended to be concentrated in certain areas

8.4. Attack on a potato store

made it all the less comprehensible to the administrators. For, faced with the famine, the British state showed its inability to cope with structural problems. In previous, small-scale famines, large sums of relief money had been directed into public works and other panaceas. But though Peel instituted some of the right kind of measures in 1846, he fell from power and Whig political economy dominated the thinking of his successors. The results were pitiful.

Irish property was supposed to meet the costs of Irish poverty; the role of the state was restricted. The market must be as far as possible undisturbed. Meanwhile the crisis reached undreamt-of proportions, with three-quarters of a million on public works by 1847. This was followed by recourse to soup-kitchens and increasing reliance on the inadequate workhouse system. By any standards (including contemporary ones), the response was inadequate. This time, the usual failure of comprehension reached tragic proportions.

8.5. A weekly meeting of the Repeal Association

The results of the famine were several. It polarised politics: O'Connell, after pleading for more wide-ranging relief measures, died in 1847 and the Repeal movement effectively died with him. Young Ireland's response was a fiasco of a revolutionary gesture: a skirmish of a Rising in a 'cabbage-patch'. The famine also accelerated economic and population developments. Population growth had already slowed, but now it plunged into decline. In the 1840s, the population declined by at least 2.5 million; about a million excess deaths, and 1.5 million emigrated. From this point, there was an Ireland abroad – in the industrial cities of Britain and North America. Here, ghetto conditions enforced a sense of identity which would later have great political importance.

The famine also helped finally to destroy the Gaelic culture of the countryside, and the language itself.[19] It also acted as a kind of Darwinian selector of the fittest landlords. Many were beggared by soaring rates in the famine years (and a few were bankrupted by their own charity, though they were exceptional). A new breed of profiteer bought up bankrupt holdings in the late 1840s (under the Encumbered Estates Act passed for the purpose in 1849), and took advantage of rural depopulation to consolidate holdings, often through eviction. Generally they looked for profit through rents, not investment, so the land problem, and the poverty problem, continued.

8.6. An eviction in southern Ireland

A political movement agitating for tenants' rights developed in the 1850s; by 1870 Gladstone was attempting to legislate for the problem, in terms suggested nearly 30 years before. At the same time, a strong tenant-farmer class had developed in the more prosperous areas, whose position was strengthened by agricultural price movements and low rents over the next generation. They would provide the last push against the landlord system from the 1880s.

Finally, the famine created a folk-memory of horror, which was exported through Young Ireland ideologues like John Mitchel, who believed (or at least wrote) that the British had deliberately planned genocide against the Irish people.[20] And in the post-famine generation, yet another secret organisation developed: the Fenians, dedicated to overthrowing the British connection by revolutionary conspiracy.

The development of a professional, internationally based revolutionary movement like Fenianism from the late 1850s might seem to be the beginning of the Irish revolution which culminated in the separatist Rising of 1916 and the ensuing guerilla war against British occupation: that is how the story used to be told. Certainly, the Fenian network organised the importation of arms, masterminded terrorist tactics, and produced some nationalist martyrs. But it also drew on that old rural secret-society tradition, which was not highly politicised and related more to local identifications and occupational diversions. Fenianism officially stressed secrecy and separatism; in practice, Fenian groups engaged in local pastimes, organised Sunday outings, drifted into constitutional politics, and were often the despair of their revolutionary leaders in France and America.[21] It was the expression of an alternative political identity, but not necessarily a separatist one. And the same can be said of the other efforts of political organisation in the post-famine years.

These culminated, in 1870, in the Home Government Association – an attempt to form a party at Westminster which would advocate a self-governing status for Ireland. It represented a variety of elements: Protestant intellectuals, irritated at Galdstone's treatment of the Church of Ireland;[22] some liberal landlords; the Catholic bourgeoisie. Fenian influence was in the background, not unfriendly. Ten years later, this rather amorphous movement would be welded into a disciplined political movement calling for Irish 'Home Rule', led by a Protestant landlord, Charles Stewart Parnell.

It would bind together many of the elements surveyed here. There was the mobilising issue of the land; the anglophobia of Irish emigrants (and their money); the implicit threat of Fenianism. It also owed much to the kind of national organisation pioneered by O'Connell, strengthened by the support of the priests. But it would also embody the contradictions that have come up again and again. It would call for 'Home Rule', a measure of self-government, without ever defining how far this meant separatism. It would raise the spectre of violence while adroitly staying within the sphere of technically constitutional action. And it would use the aspirations of the Irish middle class for acceptance in England, just as much as it manipulated the language of anti-Englishness in Ireland.

At the end of the 1780–1870 period, then, the vexed question of Ireland's relation to Britain was about to land on the table again: just as uncertain an issue as it had been at the beginning. But by now, 70 years of the Union with Britain had constricted it and the economic and social developments of the intervening period had solidified the structural divisions within Irish society.

Industrial prosperity in the north, and the advance of Catholic nationalism in the south, had set Ulster further apart than ever. The Great Famine had not only created an abiding bitterness in Irish folk memory, but had accelerated a series of changes which would eventually mean the end of landlordism in the old style. And politics had not only become inextricably mixed with religious identification, but had taken a form which owed more to O'Connellite popular organisation on the one hand, and agrarian secret-society traditions on the other, than to the class basis of democratic political evolution elsewhere.

The British imperial sense, and the agitation of Unionist interest groups in north and south, were pitted against the political dynamic of nationalism. But the development of that sense of Irish difference, and the varieties of tension with Irish society and politics, must stand out as the really important themes of the period from about 1780 to 1870.

Further reading

K.H. Connell, *The Population of Ireland 1750–1845* (Oxford, 1950); P. O'Farrell, *Ireland's English Question: Anglo-Irish relations 1534–1970* (London, 1971); J. Lee, *The Modernisation of Irish Society 1848–1918* (Dublin, 1973); O. MacDonagh, *Ireland: The Union and its Aftermath* (London, 1977); R.B. McDowell, *Ireland in the age of Imperialism and Revolution* (Oxford, 1979); G.ÕTuathaigh, *Ireland before the Famine 1798–1848 (Dublin, 1972).*

CHAPTER NINE

The View from the Colonies

David Dabydeen

In today's society of mass unemployment and creeping poverty it is
desperately difficult to recall that, only recently, Britain ruled supreme
over nearly a quarter of the earth's surface. An island of 94,000
square miles, Britain stretched herself over the whole continent of
Australia and much of North America; in the Caribbean she possessed
Trinidad, Jamaica, the Leeward and Windward Islands; in South
America, British Guiana; in Central America, British Honduras; in
Africa, she controlled countries like Sierre Leone, the Gold Coast,
Nigeria, South Africa, Rhodesia, Tanganyika, Kenya, Uganda, the
Sudan, Egypt; to the east there were India, Ceylon, Burma, Singapore
and Malaya. These countries consisted of millions of peoples from a
bewildering variety of ethnic groups, speaking a babel of different
tongues and worshipping hundreds of contradictory gods, yet they
were all contained and subdued by the imperial yoke. The fact that a
tiny minority of British citizens could subjugate a vast country like,
say, India, was cause for wonder; in the words of a recent historian,
the conquest of India 'remains one of the remarkable events of
modern history'.[1] In 1833, Macaulay, reflecting on the British control
of India, marvelled at the achievement:

> that a handful of adventurers from an island in the Atlantic should
> have subjugated a vast country divided from the place of their birth
> by half the globe . . . that we should govern a territory . . . larger
> and more populous than France, Spain, Italy and Germany put
> together . . . a territory inhabited by men differing from us in race,
> colour, langue, manners, morals, religion – these are prodigies to
> which the world has seen nothing similar.[2]

Today, Britain owns a few disappearing specks of land on the globe, and the nation is depressed, but at the height of empire her citizens were giddy with a sense of political, economic, cultural and religious supremacy. 'Rule Britannia, Britannia rules the waves' was the rallying cry of the nation. The world, it appeared, existed to supply and service British needs. Britain was the Mother Country, with a brood of colonies in her care who were to be persuaded and, whenever necessary, chastised, towards the path of economic development and civilisation.

The establishment of colonies was due to several factors. Religious tyranny in Britain led to several christian sects emigrating in search of distant havens. Puritans, Quakers, Congregationalists, Catholics and others fled the restrictions and persecutions of the established church to settle in America and the Caribbean. In the case of the Irish, poverty and famine combined with ruthless religious oppression to drive them to foreign lands. Between 1750 and 1800 alone, an estimated 200,000 Irish citizens emigrated to America.[3] If they provided refuge for paupers and disaffected christians, the colonies were also used as a dumping ground for Britain's criminal population. A succession of royal decrees and parliamentary Acts empowered the judiciary to order the transportation of criminals to the colonies. Those convicted of robbery, prostitution, burglary and other felonies were bound to seven years servitude in the colonies; if their crimes were punishable by the death sentence, they could instead be bound to 14 years labour, at the expiry of which contract of service, they would become free men. Often the crimes of these people were extremely

9.1. The transportation of prisoners to Australia

petty – in the eighteenth century the theft of a silver spoon could lead to transportation. In the nineteenth century trade union activity was punishable by transportation. Transportation became an organised business: men such as John Stewart, who were contracted to organise the shipping of criminals to the colonies made decent livings from these human indecencies. Stewart was paid £5.00 for every convict he shipped, which included an allowance for food during the voyage, the cost of leg irons, chains and handcuffs. Between 1729 and 1770, sometimes as high a proportion as 70 per cent of defendants convicted at the Old Bailey were sentenced to transporation.[4] It is certain that magistrates would receive bribes from shipping agents such as Stewart to find people guilty. Usually they ended up in America and the Caribbean, but after the American Revolution Australia became the favourite open jail. In 1786 the Home Secretary, Lord Sidney, announced that the British government would henceforth banish its criminals to Australia. Between 1787 and 1868, when the system of transportation was abolished, over 150,000 convicts were exported to Australia. People from other parts of the British Empire were also sentenced to penal servitude in Australia, the country serving as an international jail. After the Morant Bay Rebellion in Jamaica in 1865, when the people rioted against British abuses, many Jamaicans ended up in Australia.

Apart from the usefulness of colonies as a dumping ground for religious or criminal outcasts from Britain, the main reason for their establishment was for commercial profit. The colonies provided Britain with an abundance of raw materials like sugar, cotton, tea, tobacco, timber, spices, dyes and naval stores. They were in turn outlets for British manufactured goods, and new markets for British trade. It was a vastly unequal relationship. Manufacturing was strictly the monopoly of Britain. The role of the colonies was merely to provide the raw material for British science and industry. Between 1854 and 1857, 85.1 per cent of the volume of Britain's exports were in manufactured goods and 61.2 per cent in raw materials.[5] The country was thus deeply dependent on supplies from overseas territories. Throughout the eighteenth century and the first two decades of the nineteenth century the West Indies were considered to be the jewels of the empire. The West Indies were the major source of imports to Great Britain, producing a greater value of raw materials than Asia or America combined. Sugar was the most precious commodity, grown by hundreds of thousands of slaves shipped from West Africa. The African was seen as indispensable to the labour-intensive demands of the plantation economy. 'Negroes', one plantation owner wrote, 'are the sinews of a plantation, and it is impossible for a man to make sugar without the assistance of the negroes, as to make bricks without straw.'[6] In the area of the slave trade perhaps as many as 15 million Africans were carried by European ships to the New World colonies, the British having a substantial share in the shipping of slaves.[7] The slave trade was an enormously lucrative business and it was crucial to the maintenance of world commerce. In eighteenth-century opinion, the slave trade was 'the spring and parent whence the others flow', 'the first principle of foundation of all the rest, the main spring of the machine which sets every wheel in motion'.[8]

The British justified this trade on the grounds that the African was not a human being, but more in the nature of an animal. Lord Chesterfield for instance, in one of his famous letters to his son, wrote that 'Africans are little better than the lions, tigers, and other wild beasts, that that continent produces in such horrible numbers. It is thus acceptable to buy them in Africa and to sell them for profit in the West Indies'.[9] Lord Grosvenor, arguing in Parliament against the abolition of the slave trade, agreed that the trade was 'an unamiable trade', but added, with no recognition of the callousness of its comparison, that 'so also were many others. The trade of a butcher was an unamiable trade, but it was a very necessary one not withstanding.'[10] The processing of blacks and of mutton was obviously identical. This definition of Africans as subhuman justified their physical beating; William Knox, in a pamphlet written for the Society for the Propagation of the Gospel, could openly state, 'it is no wonder that they are treated like brute beasts. If they are incapable of feeling mentally, they will the more frequently be made to feel in their flesh.'[11] The slave trade is replete with examples of barbarities and episodes of genocide. One of the most heartless and revealing incidents in the history of the trade concerned the slave ship *Zong*. In September 1781, the ship, loaded with 470 African slaves, set off for Jamaica. Two months later, 60 of the slaves had died, the others were sick, with many on the brink of death, and Jamaica was still a far way off. The ship's captain, worried about the drop in value of his human cargo, decided to cut his loss by dumping 133 slaves overboard and claiming their insurance value instead. The slaves who were sickest and most unlikely to survive the voyage were gathered together in batches and systematically thrown overboard. On the first day, 54 were dumped, on the second day, 43. One slave managed miraculously to cling on to a rope and climb back on to the ship secretly, where he hid successfully, only to be discovered and sold on his arrival in Jamaica. On the third day the remaining 36 slaves put up a fight and had to be shackled before being drowned. The shipowners claimed compensation from the insurers and though the insurers argued in court against the legality of the claim, the court ordered that they should pay it. Abolitionists like Granville Sharp called for the trial of the captain and crew for mass murder, but the solicitor general argued that morality was irrelevant in a case concerned purely with property rights:

> This is a case of chattels or goods. It is really so; it is the case of throwing over goods; for to this purpose, and the purpose of the insurance, they are goods and property; whether right or wrong, we have nothing to do with.[12]

The dividends to be reaped from the slave trade and from slave-produced commodities blinded people to moral issues. The fortunes amassed were enormous and contributed directly to the economic development of Britain, and to the phenomenal growth of its cities. At the end of the seventeenth century, Liverpool was an insignificant seaport, a mere village, with a few rough streets and a few hundred households. By the end of the eighteenth century, its population had increased fifteenfold and its shipping activities made it one of the world's great seaports. This extraordinary evolution was due to the slave trade. By the end of the eighteenth century, Liverpool's ships were responsible for some 60 per cent of the British trade in slaves. One contemporary estimated that between 1783 and 1793 some 304,000 slaves valued at over £15 million were carried in 878 Liverpool ships.[13] An eighteenth-century Liverpool ballad summed up its dependence on slavery thus:

9.2. Liverpool in the seventeenth century

9.3. Liverpool: a
bustling port by 1840

If our slave trade had gone, there is an end to our lives,
Beggars all we must be, our children and wives:
No ships from our ports their proud sails ere would spread,
And our streets grown with grass, where the cows might be fed.[14]

Bristol too became a big city as a result of slavery and slave-
produced commodities. In 1833, one Bristol merchant admitted that
without West Indian commerce his city would have remained a mere
fishing port. The transportation of slaves to the West Indies and of
sugar from the West Indies accounted for the bulk of its shipping, and
transformed Bristol from a small town into Britain's second city.
Dozens of ancillary trades sprang up to service the slave business.
Rope-making, barrel-making, ship-building and ship-repairing employed thousands of workers, and thousands of others were engaged
as sailors. Banking and insurance services, to facilitate the commercial
operation of slavery, also received a tremendous boost. The Bank of
England was dominated by West Indian interests, with many of its
directors and governors throughout the eighteenth century being
deeply implicated in slavery. Some, like Humphrey Morice, governor
of the Bank of England between 1727 and 1729, actually owned slave
ships; others, like Sir Richard Neave, director of the bank for 48 years
and governor between 1783 and 1785, had substantial personal

investments in West Indian commerce. Neave was chairman of the Society of West Indian Merchants. Other individuals who made fortunes from dealing in slaves launched their own banks. Thomas Leyland, mayor of Liverpool in 1798, 1814 and 1820, owner of several slave ships, became so rich that he started a bank in 1807 which soon accumulated assets of over £1 million. The bank flourished throughout the nineteenth century. Assets were absorbed into the North and South Wales Bank in 1901, which in turn was taken over by the Midland Bank. David and Alexander Barclay, founders of Barclays Bank, were slave-traders in the 1750s. David Barclay also owned a wealthy slave plantation in Jamaica. As to the world of insurance, businesses like Lloyds, which was once a mere coffee house in London, became giant household names as a result of slavery and colonial trade. At the end of the seventeenth century, Lloyds coffee house was the location for the auction of ships trading in America and the West Indies. In the following century, it insured slaves and slave ships as well as buildings in the West Indies. One of its most distinguished chairmen in the nineteenth century was Joseph Marryat, a West Indian planter who owned 391 slaves in Trinidad and Jamaica.[15]

British industry also benefited from slavery. Birmingham became a major exporter of firearms to Africa: between 1796 and 1805 an annual average of 161,551 guns were shipped to Africa, guns which were exchanged for slaves and which maintained control of the slaves. Towns like Swansea benefited enormously by becoming wholesale suppliers of copper goods to slave-merchants. Slave-grown cotton fed the spinning machines of Manchester, making that city one of the world's largest exporters of cloth. In 1788, the cloth trade gave employment to 180,000 men, women and children, a figure that was greatly increased in the next century.

Perhaps the most spectacular instance of the relationship between industry and slavery concerns the steam engine of James Watt. The invention and building of the steam engine in the 1770s was financed by a bank whose capital came from the West Indian trade.[16] The steam engine in turn became the driving force of Britain's industrial revolution, working the manufacturing mills and factories that made Britain the world's supreme industrialised nation. In the colonies, the steam train and steam boat opened up hitherto closed or unexplored regions, creating vast new markets for British goods. In the 1830s, one British explorer of Africa, writing about the relationship between steam and empire, declared:

We have the power in our hands, moral, physical, and mechanical; the first, based on the Bible; the second, upon the wonderful adaptation of the Anglo-Saxon race to all climates, situations, and circumstances; and third, bequeathed to us by the immortal Watt. By his invention every river is laid open to us, time and distance are shortened.[17]

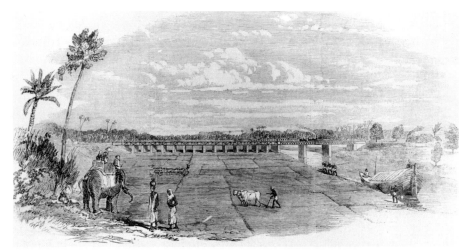

9.4. The British take the railway to India: Sursuttee Bridge and Aqueduct

British domination of the world thus netted her capital for commercial and industrial growth. It was, however, a domination fiercely resisted by the native peoples of that empire. In the West Indies, slave revolts on the plantations were endemic. Only by the most brutal methods of punishment and mass executions did the British suppress these rebellions. Slaves also ran away and formed independent communities in remote areas from which they would engage in guerrilla raids upon the British. In India, the most horrific instance of resistance to British rule took place between 1857–8. By then, India was considered the jewel of the empire. The West Indies were no longer of pre-eminent economic importance to Britain, the sugar plantations being in decline due to free trade competition from French colonial sugar and to soil exhaustion. India became crucial to British commerce since it was the largest single market for British cotton goods. It was also the second largest market for all British manufactured goods. Under British rule India, once an exporter of cloth to Britain, was turned into a major importer, its cotton industry unprotected against the cheap flood of British machine-made cloth. The British attempted to consolidate their economic stranglehold of the country by cultural propaganda. Missionaries interfered with local religions and religious practices in their attempt to convert people to christianity. A series of social, agricultural and economic measures was initiated, all aimed at reforming or abolishing traditional Indian customs and institutions. The overall intention was to make India more manageable and economically exploitable by converting it to

British ways. The resulting disaffection led to a mutiny by the Indian army, who turned their guns against their British officers. The military mutiny sparked off massive civil rebellions in many provinces of India. Both sides indulged in atrocities. The rebels, upon capturing a town, would massacre its white population, including women and children. The British in turn, on capturing a rebel stronghold, would murder the Indians in hundreds. The Indians were shot, hanged out of hand, burnt alive and blown from guns by the British. It was racial war on an horrendous scale, an explosion of racial hatred which finally gave the lie to British claims about the benevolence and civilising nature of their empire.[18]

9.5. Bones of mutineers in a courtyard at Lucknow

The struggle against empire did not take place only in the colonies, but in Britain itself. During the era of the slave trade, several thousand blacks were brought over to England by retiring planters and by ship's captains, to work in private households. One newspaper in 1780 estimated that there were 20,000 blacks in London alone.

From this community of blacks emerged leaders of national prominence who were in the forefront of early British trade union agitation. One of the leaders of the Cato Street conspiracy, which was a plot to assassinate the whole of the British cabinet as it met at a dinner in Grosvenor Square, was a black man, William Davidson.[19] In 1819, Davidson joined a group of radical shoemakers and was elected secretary of their trade union. The union was appalled by the recent

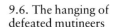
9.6. The hanging of defeated mutineers

Peterloo massacre, when class war had broken out in the streets of Manchester. A peaceful demonstration by the working people of Lancashire had been broken up by soldiers who charged into the helpless crowd wielding sabres. Eleven people, including two women and a child, were killed and several hundred injured. The massacre, condemned by a majority of the population, was condoned by the government, who openly congratulated the officers involved. Davidson's union believed that further similar peaceful protest would be savagely crushed, and therefore decided upon the drastic action of wiping out the cabinet. Davidson was delegated to purchase the arms for this prospect, and the subsequent uprising. He bought 450 muskets and 2700 rounds of ammunition. The plot was, however, foiled at the last minute and Davidson, together with four white ringleaders, was publicly hanged, then beheaded, in 1820. It was the last public decapitation in England.

Davidson's radicalism was fired by a sense of the racial injustice done to blacks all over the world under the British colonial system, and he saw a parallel class injustice in Britain; hence his sympathy for the white working classes. Working-class and trade union agitation in the early nineteenth century frequently allied itself to the cause of black liberation. Socialist pamphlets of the age made appeals to the white working classes, urging them to recognise in the suffering of African slaves the conditions of their own suffering. Many of the leading radical reformers of the period were also active abolitionists. The Abolition Movement in the late eighteenth and early nineteenth centuries was the first mass philanthropic movement in Britain, with millions of people from all over the kingdom signing parliamentary petitions for the ending of the slave trade. The working-class radicalism of the nineteenth century had its roots in the Abolition Movement. British socialism grew partly out of the mass experience of campaigning for the liberation of blacks.

An excellent example of black struggle in alliance with white working-class protest can be found in the case of William Cuffay. Cuffay, originally the son of a West Indian slave, ended up as one of the leaders and martyrs of the Chartist movement in Britain, which was 'the first mass political movement of the British working classes'. The Chartists wanted reform of corruptions in the voting system, whereby the wealthy could buy their way into Parliament. Only those who owned property could vote and the Chartists wanted the vote extended to the poor. Cuffay, a tailor by trade, plunged himself into trade union activity, and suffered attacks from the press. The satirical journal *Punch*, for instance, repeatedly ridiculed his efforts. In 1848 Cuffay was appointed chairman of a committee appointed to organise a mass rally to Parliament. The rally was to present a petition bearing nearly a million signatures. The authorities banned the march and made extensive defence plans. Peter Fryer, a modern historian, describes how:

> the queen had been packed off to the Isle of Wight for her safety, and the royal carriages and horses and other valuables had been removed from the palace. Tens of thousands of lawyers, shop-keepers, and government clerks had been enrolled as special constables. All government buildings were prepared for attack: at the Foreign Office, the ground floor windows were blocked with bound volumes of *The Times*, thought to be thick enough to stop bullets, and the clerks were issued with brand-new service muskets and ball cartridges. The British Museum was provided with 50 muskets and 100 cutlasses. The Bank of England was protected with sandbags. Along the Embankment, 7,000 soldiers were distributed at strategic points. Heavy gun batteries were brought up from Woolwich. The bridges were sealed off and guarded by over 4,000 police.[20]

Cuffay was subsequently arrested and put on trial on the charge of levying war against Queen Victoria. He was transported to Australia on a life sentence and he died in a workhouse in Tasmania. His political activities in London, despised by the establishment, were warmly admired by other more honest commentators. In 1849 Thomas Wheeler, writing in the newspaper, the *Northern Star*, recalled how, at a political meeting in the 1840s, he first:

gazed with unfeigned admiration upon the high intellectual forehead and animated features of this dimunitive Son of Africa's despised and injured race. Though the son of a West Indian and the grandson of an African slave, he spoke the English tongue pure and grammatical, and with a degree of ease and facility which would shame many who boast of the purity of their Saxon or Norman descent. Possessed of attainments superior to the majority of working men, he had filled, with honour, the highest offices of his trade society.[21]

The reference to Cuffay's eloquence, intellect and learning is profoundly relevant, for among the greatest achievements of black people in the Era of Empire was the literature they produced. Several slave narratives were written in the eighteenth and nineteenth centuries by black West Indians, black Americans and black British. Some slaves learned to read and write through the missionary effort to teach them the Bible. Other slaves secretly stole books from the libraries of their masters and taught themselves to read English. Ignatius Sancho, for instance, a famous black writer in eighteenth-century Britain, described how 'I was placed in a family who judged ignorance the best and only security for obedience. A little reading and writing I got by unwearied application.'[22]

9.7. Portrait of Olaudah Equiano

Perhaps the most accomplished of the slave narrators was Olaudah Equiano, who published his autobiography in England in 1789.[23] Equiano's book is critical for two reasons: firstly, it draws an authentic picture of Ibo society remembered from childhood days. European explorers may have described Africa as a land of unspeakable barbarities, but Equiano's Africa is ordered and regulated, the society bound together by laws and humanistic cultural customs:

We are almost a nation of dancers, musicians and poets. Thus every great event such as a triumphant return from battle or other cause of public rejoicing is celebrated in public dances, which are accompanied with songs and music. . . . When our women are not employed with the men in tillage, their usual occupation is spinning and weaving cotton, which they afterwards dye and make into garments. They also manufacture earthen vessels of which we have many kinds. . . . Before we taste food we always wash our hands: indeed our cleanliness on all occasions is extreme, but on this it is an indispensable ceremony. After washing, libation is made by pouring out a small portion of the drink on the floor, and tossing a small quantity of the food in a certain place for the spirits of departed relations, which the natives suppose to preside over their conduct and guard them from evil. They are totally unacqainted with strong or spirituous liquors, and their principal beverage is palm wine. Everyone contributes something to the common stock, and as we are unacquainted with idleness, we have no beggars.

These descriptions from within sweep away the racist myths and stereotypes about African behaviour that had accumulated in white literature. Secondly, Equiano gives us unique insight into how blacks perceived the white intruders in their midst. Captured on the coast and put on board a slaveship, he is terrified that the whites intend to eat the cargo of slaves. He turns to some of his fellow captives and asks them 'if we are not to be eaten by those white men with horrible looks, red faces, and loose hair'. In other words, it was *the blacks* who saw the white newcomers as cannibals. On the voyage to Barbados, Equiano is constantly terrified by the primitive behaviour of the white crew towards the blacks and towards each other:

> The white people looked and acted, as I thought, in so savage a manner; for I had never seen among my people such instances of brutal cruelty, and this is not only shewn towards us blacks but also to some of the whites themselves. One white man in particular I saw, when we were permitted to be on deck, flogged so unmercifully with a large rope near the foremast that he died in consequence of it; and they tossed him over the side as they would have done a brute. This made me fear these people the more, and I expected nothing less than to be treated in the same manner.

On landing in Barbados, the greed of the slave marketeers again confirms his suspicion that whites are barbarians:

> On a signal given (as the beat of a drum) the buyers rush at once into the yard where the slaves are confined, and make choice of that parcel they like best. The noise and clamour with which this is attended and the eagerness visible in the countenances of the buyers serve not a little to increase the apprehensions of the terrified Africans, who may well be supposed to consider them as the ministers of that destruction to which they think themselves devoted.

Throughout the narrative, Equiano genuinely struggles to find examples which would redeem white people from universal condemnation as savages, but he is constantly disappointed by their lack of imagination and lack of moral idealism. The book is extremely well written: its wit, its moral calmness and its humility of tone revealing a deeply intelligent and compassionate man. It was an eighteenth-century bestseller – between 1789 and 1827 it went into 17 editions in Britain and America, and was translated into Dutch and German. Equiano became famous in England as a leading campaigner for the abolition of slavery, travelling all over the kingdom to address crowded public meetings. He led several black delegations to the House of Commons to attend the slavery debates. He was received by the Speaker of the House and by the Prime Minister. Equiano was a black missionary in darkest England, trying to convert the natives here to common decencies and civilised ways.

One eighteenth-century slave ship captain, John Newton, describing his cargo, had written that 'the slaves lie in two rows, one above the other . . . like books upon a shelf. I have known them so close that the shelf would not easily contain one more.'[24] This library image reveals the crucial paradox of slavery – the fact that the barbaric business was conducted by gentlemen of taste and learning. With Equiano and other writers, blacks moved from being packed like books aboard the slaveship to being the authors of books. It was a profound transformation, achieved by the will to resist savagery, and the will to persuade their imperial masters to civilised behaviour. The true heroism of empire was not the boldness of the white explorers or the courage of the white soldiers and administrators so celebrated in nineteenth-century boys' adventure tales. The true heroism of empire was displayed by its subject peoples, in their will to survive and to triumph over the barbarity that was the British Empire.

Further reading

R.T. Anstey 'Capitalism and Slavery: A Critique', *Economic History Review*, 2nd Series, XXI (1968), 307–20; G.D. Bearce, *British Attitudes towards India 1784–1858* (London, 1961); D. Dabydeen (ed.), *The Black Presence in English Literature* (Manchester University Press, 1985); Peter Fryer, *Staying Power: The History of Black People in Britain* (London, 1984); G.S. Graham, *A Concise History of the British Empire* (London, 1970); R. Hyam, *Britain's Imperial Century 1815–1914* (London, 1976); E. Williams, *Capitalism and Slavery* (Chapel Hill, 1944).

CHAPTER TEN

A Week at the Seaside

James Walvin

By the late nineteenth century, the British people enjoyed a range of leisure and recreational facilities which their forebears could scarcely have dreamed of. Indeed many of the mass enjoyments of the modern world were well-established features of British life by the 1890s. Modern soccer was played by thousands and watched by millions; cricket too was a popular, participatory and spectator sport. In fact there was a host of games and sports which were newly-codified, nationwide and immensely popular – in schools, in commercial stadiums and in more informal settings – on open spaces, in streets and parks. This was true of tennis, athletics, rowing and rugby (of both varieties). Moreover all of these sports – and more besides – were at the same time being rapidly adopted in a great number of different societies around the world. Black South Africans played football, the descendants of slaves swiftly took up cricket throughout the Caribbean and of course white settlements around the world turned to the leisures of their 'Mother Country' – Britain.[1]

It is no coincidence that the modern Olympic movement was launched in 1896, by a French aristocrat, the Baron de Coubertin, anxious to promote on a world stage the qualities he detected in the athleticism within British public schools. And yet, for all the spreading internationalism of sports and recreations, it was the *British* who saw themselves as, and prided themselves in being, a particularly sporting people. Indeed 'playing the game' had by the late century become an ethical code which was thought to be applicable to all forms of social activity.[2]

It would be wrong, however, to concentrate on sports. What is striking to the observer of the late nineteenth century is the extraordinary range and diversity of all forms of leisure activities: for all ages, all social classes and for both sexes. These years witnessed the emergence of a variety of recreational pursuits and sports which, though familiar to the modern reader, were relatively new developments in the social life of the British people. Organised holidays, notably the mass exodus from urban areas on the bank holidays (introduced in 1871), the epic and (to foreigners at least) the perplexing rush to the seaside resorts in the summer season, these and a host of new or reformed games and leisure pursuits collectively transformed the social lives of the British people. This was especially striking among working people, growing numbers of whom were able to enjoy many of the newer material benefits disgorged by the mature British economy by virtue of their increased (though none the less limited) purchasing power. Moreover, there were wide sections of working-class life, notably those men in the heavier basic industries, whose working conditions were protected by powerful trade unions, and who found themselves with free time – leisure time – in which to enjoy their favourite recreations or sports. Football, like the seaside trip, the committal to choral and brass band music-making, the growing cult of gardening and allotments, or the mass proliferation of music halls throughout urban Britain – all these and more were, in essence, functions of fundamental changes in the economic life of the nation. Although each element in the complicated history of the development of modern leisure provides an interesting and colourful story in itself, what is perhaps most revealing is the way the history of leisure offers a telling insight into the fundamental economic and social changes which came to transform the face of urban Britain.[3]

Few recreations were more popular, more ubiquitous, and more representative of major social changes, than football. It was a game which, in the space of a generation, emerged from the reformed English public schools to become the passion of urban working men throughout England and Scotland. By the end of the century it had developed a similar following throughout the world. Not surprisingly, the passions, the noise, the crowds and the mass obsessions of football had their critics. For example, the periodical the *Ethical World* was highly critical of football and its supporters but was, nevertheless, a major advocate of working-class leisure, but in a healthier and more wholesome environment than the urban areas which spawned the dominant working-class pleasures: 'The more sensible members of the working-class drift away from the city on one or other of the innumerable day-excursions – to Brighton or Southend, or to homes and friends in provincial towns.' Many, it was claimed, flocked to the local parks and open spaces in their holiday breaks but: 'Of the great residue that hovers all day about the music-halls and public houses of the city let us be silent, conscience-striken.'[4]

What concerned large numbers of late-century social critics was that

10.1. A football match

football had become a reflection of a host of unattractive character-
istics of urban life. Where the game had once been promoted as a
healthy and disciplined recreation for working men whose lives were,
by and large, blighted by the miseries of city life, it had by 1900
become a highly commercialised weekly ritual, which encouraged
passionate, local (often religious) fanaticism, collective and vulgar
rowdiness and a general plebeian assertiveness which seemed (to
outsiders at least) undesirably divisive in an already divided nation.
For good or ill, football had sunk its roots deep into urban, especially
working-class, life long before the end of Victoria's reign. Furthermore, for all the criticism which was directed (often unfairly) at
football in those years, the game's defenders and proponents were no
less vociferous and assertive. Of course, what gave the game its unique
hold over so many people was its fundamental appeal to players and
spectators alike. Easy and enjoyable to play – encouraged from early
years in the new Board schools – enjoyable to watch, accessible to
even the meanest of urban communities, rooted in local institutions
(churches, Sunday schools, factories and trade unions), football was,
with certain regional exceptions, the undisputed game of working-
class life. In the words of one commentator in 1895: 'The nation, we
are told, is a democracy, and the game of the people must be accepted
as the game of the nation.' Though the game's critics were many and
aggressive, there could be no denying its following. 'No words of
ours', wrote one man in 1886, 'can adequately describe the present
popularity of football with the public – a popularity which, though
great in metropolis, is infinitely greater in the large provincial towns.'[5]
This sketch of football in 1900 is offered not simply as an example

of the broader story of late-century leisure, but as an extraordinary contrast to the position 70 years earlier. At Victoria's death, the variety and importance of her subjects' recreations and mass pleasures formed a remarkable contrast to the paucity of leisure at the time of her accession. Where the provision and enjoyments of leisure were rich and vibrant by the late nineteenth century, they had been sparse, restricted and socially limited at the beginning of the century. Indeed there were few more dramatic changes in the social lives of nineteenth-century British people than the transformation of their leisure patterns.

By the 1830s various observers of British life frequently remarked on the dearth of recreations for the common people. Of course for people of substance – the leisured class for whom free time and money posed no significant problem – there survived that rich and varied social life which had long characterised the London season and the periodic migrations to the spa towns or rural retreats. But their pleasures – of the field or theatre, the assembly rooms, libraries, or the colourful world of domestic social entertainment – were, naturally enough, restricted to the confines of their social equals. There was, it is true, a certain social mingling at play, between the worlds of old and new money, between traditional landed wealth and that created by the opportunities of trade, enterprise and overseas expansion: perhaps best illustrated by the social life at Bath. There, in the words of Smollett:

> Every upstart of fortune, harnessed to the trappings of the mode, presents himself at Bath. . . . Clerks and factors from the East Indies, loaded with the spoil of plundered provinces; planters, negro-drivers and hucksters from the American plantations, enriched they know not how . . . all of them hurry to Bath, because here, without any further qualification, they can mingle with the princes and the nobles of the land.[6]

By and large however, the bulk of ordinary working people could merely watch and perhaps envy the pleasurable cavortings of their social betters. They were, as they had always been, as remote from the pleasures of their betters as they were distant from them in other walks of life, and for the same harsh, economic reasons. People's access to leisure was determined and shaped in large part by economic and social circumstance. True, the overriding need to scratch a meagre living from a generally hostile environment was interrupted by traditional pleasures: Christmas, Easter, Shrove Tuesday, feast days, local fairs and festivals, parish ceremonies and the like. It is also the case that there was no clear dividing line between work and play; time

10.2. Promenading at
Bath

could generally be found to escape to the nearest attraction. But this
changed quite dramatically with the encroachment of first urban and
then mechanical, industrial life (though we must not exaggerate the
numbers involved in modern industry up to mid century).[7]

Even before this took place, however, there developed a concerted
attack on popular pleasures by certain men of property. Just as in the
seventeenth century, these men demanded a new social discipline and
insisted that many of the older, turbulent and often violent pleasures
give way to more refined, 'rational' pleasures. The determination to
produce a 'refinement of manners' was part of the drive to shape a
new social discipline. Large crowds, drunkenness, blood sports,
boxing, pleasurable activities on the Sabbath – all these and more
were seen as subversive of good social order.[8] This was particularly
acute in an age when a growing proportion of the population found
themselves living in urban areas. The disciplines of town life – later of
industrial life – required a new personal and collective discipline, and
one which was hostile to the traditional recreations of the common
people. Local urban rules, pressure groups – and legislation – sought
to curb the old pleasures and to encourage the pursuit of more
disciplined, more rational recreations. Yet the survival of so many
'traditional' enjoyments, ancient fairs in the heart of London in the
1860s for example, is testimony to the durability of old popular
culture and, of course, of their persistent popularity among the
common people. Historians have often emphasised the break, the
discontinuity, between the popular leisures of the modern and the old
pre-industrial world. It now seems clear, however, that many survived,
often in transmuted form, well into the nineteenth century and
beyond.

More important than the efforts of men of property to change popular leisure were the forces of urban and economic change and their consequences for leisure pursuits. Two factors in particular conspired to produce such changes; increasing restrictions on free time, and changes in physical space. Traditional open spaces – places where recreations had taken place since time out of mind – were consumed by urban growth. Even in rural communities, the common lands succumbed to enclosure and rural economic change. In addition, the growing mechanisation of life and the encroachment of a new discipline which was itself dictated by the clock and the needs of the machine, recast the nature of spare time. For those people engaged in mechanical operations, however indirectly, free time became an increasingly scarce commodity. Moreover the Sabbath was fiercely protected by Sabbatarians. Thus urban people of the mid nineteenth century found themselves with reduced access to recreational space and time compared with many of their forebears.

However, such restraints were no impediment to the prosperous, who were growing in numbers with the economic advance of the nation and for whom there developed an increasingly varied round of pleasure pursuits during the London season and at the spa towns that proliferated in the seventeenth and eighteenth centuries. At Bath, Tunbridge Wells, Scarborough, Harrogate and elsewhere a highly sophisticated calendar of fashionable and costly pleasures and rituals was available. The great bulk of the people could only watch and envy their betters as they cavorted through their expensive pleasures. Yet paradoxically it was the changes which came over these spa towns which heralded a major transformation – a democratisation – of the leisures of the common people. And if we wish to see the manner in which old pleasures subtly adapted themselves to the rapid changes of the nineteenth century we need look no further than the history of 'taking the waters'. From the seventeenth century onwards the inland spas had established their fame not merely for the curative powers of their mineral waters but also for those activities they provided for their prosperous visitors. Charles Wesley thought Bath 'The headquarters of Satan' but its popularity as a leisure centre grew steadily. But Bath, like other spas, was socially exclusive. Within a very brief period, however, 'taking the waters' became a major, national leisure pursuit for all classes of British people.[9]

The beginnings of that change can be traced to Brighton where in the mid-eighteenth century Dr Russell established a medical *régime* of taking not mineral but local *sea*water. To drink and bathe in the seawater soon established itself as a fashionable medical and social *régime*, confirmed by royalty and aristocracy and swiftly propagated as a fashionable fad. The urban growth of Brighton, improved roads

10.3. The Pump Room
at Bath

and transport from London, and a similar development of resorts on the Thames estuary (and the ease of travelling there by boat) all helped to secure for these new seaside resorts a remarkable and quite unexpected popularity. In the north, Scarborough similarly developed its appeal but – as with the southern resorts – it did so initially and primarily for people of substance. In general the resorts modelled themselves specifically on the older, inland mineral water spas: in clientele, architecture, social provision and medical appeal. But what transformed them utterly was the coming of the railways. Here, as in so many other areas of British social history, the railways proved to be a powerful agent in the democratisation of British life, in rendering more available, more widespread and accessible, facilities previously enjoyed only by a privileged minority.[10]

Throughout the 1840s the new railway companies forged links between the inland urban areas and the embryonic resorts and ports. In some cases resorts came into being *because* of the presence of railway links: Rhyll and Bournemouth for example. Whenever a new railway link was opened to the coast, it was swiftly followed by accounts of working people descending on the newly accessible coastal spot, encouraged by the railway companies' development of excursion trips and cheap fares. This was precisely what local objectors had feared: the opening of their previously exclusive town to mass invasion and large-scale pleasure-seeking. Writing of Blackpool in 1841, the *Preston Pilot* bemoaned:

Unless immediate steps are taken, Blackpool as a resort for respectable visitors will be ruined. . . . Unless the cheap trains are discontinued or some effective regulation made for the management of the thousands who visit the place, Blackpool property will be depreciated past recovery.

Much the same story was told of Scarborough where opposition to the

10.4. The beginnings of seaside development at Brighton

excursion trains came from those 'with no wish for a greater influx of vagrants, and those who have no money to spend'.[11] Their worst dreams were realised and within a month of opening the railways delivered the first excursionists from Wakefield and Newcastle. The queen herself moved from Brighton in 1841; she later retreated to the fastness of Balmoral.

There thus developed a social tone to the resorts. Some tried to remain propertied: upper or middle class. Some sought to keep out the trains or to prevent the use of local land for the kind of development needed for popular excursionists' recreations. Others committed themselves to the development of a plebian style and appeal in their local entertainments, while still others, Scarborough for instance, were able through careful zoning to remain attractive to various social classes.[12] By the late century, the seaside resorts had, like so many other types of British towns and cities, come to represent class and social differences. At play as at work, the British were divided by social class.

Perhaps *the* most striking feature of the seaside resorts was their rate of growth, which was greater than any other type of town. Between 1811 and 1851 the largest resorts recorded a population growth of an astonishing 214 per cent. Not even the largest industrial towns came close to this figure. Of course the resorts were never as *big* as the industrial towns – Brighton's population in 1851 for example was only 65,000 – but their *rate* of growth was significantly greater. It is moreover worth remembering that of the nine major resorts at half-century only three – Scarborough, Whitby and Blackpool – were in the North. By the twentieth century upwards of 150 towns claimed to be resorts, though inevitably they ranged from the tiniest and often crudest of seaside villages, to the major seaside towns which could by then boast some of the most varied and sophisticated of urban facilities, both for residents and for visitors.[13]

It was then at the resorts and in travelling to and from the resorts, that there developed that quintessentially British phenomenon – the seaside holiday. It is worth dwelling on this phenomenon in some detail; to consider who went to the seaside, what they did when they were there, in order to come to terms with some of the basic changes in the broader patterns of contemporary leisure patterns.

Geography was important. After all, no part of inland Britain was more than 70 miles from the coast. But proximity alone cannot explain why people from one area chose to visit, on a regular and recurring basis, particular resorts. Leeds for instance is as close to Blackpool as it is to Scarborough. But local working people gravitated to the Yorkshire and not the Lancashire coast. Similarly London's population was lured to the resorts along the Thames estuary – Southend, Gravesend and Margate – and to resorts on the Kent and Sussex coast. East Midlanders preferred the Lincolnshire and Norfolk coasts; others travelled to North Wales. There were, it is true, increasing exceptions to these general patterns as the century advanced and as consumer power grew and railway lines proliferated. But the key to many of these patterns was transportation. Initially at least, railway links were crucial in guiding travelling working people towards particular resorts. In London, travelling down the Thames helps to explain the developing popularity of the estuary towns.

Railway and steamer travel was however, to no avail without the financial wherewithal to benefit from it. Here – and in common with other forms of popular leisure in the nineteenth century – we confront the crucial importance of changing economic fortunes. Historians continue to argue about the standards of living of working people in the years up to mid century. Thereafter, however, and not withstanding the local, trade, personal or temporal exceptions, working people began to gain some of the material benefits of an industrialising nation. Spare cash may have been meagre, and often precariously maintained, but it was available to ever more working people. They could spend it on the expanding range of consumer goods and indeed much spare cash went into buying those items which were actively improving the conditions of domestic material life. But large numbers of working people were also able, and willing, to set aside some cash for a trip – albeit for only a day – to the seaside.[14] Certain groups of working people were more prominent than others at the seaside:

young, unattached males for instance. But what made the seaside trip doubly attractive to so many working people was the fact that it established itself as a *family* affair. Most other leisures were shaped by sexual as well as social divides, but the seaside offered a range of natural and man-made pleasures for all the family, young and old, male and female. Indeed surviving photographic evidence illustrates this point perfectly.

What established the resort so firmly in the popular imagination was the experience of childhood. From the early days of the trains, excursions were organised by Sunday Schools, churches, factories and

10.5. The new fashion for swimming

local benefactors and charitable organisations to take children away from the grime of their urban habitat to the pleasures and fresh air of the coast. More privileged children experienced similar delights when their parents went for more extensive visits – to apartments, hotels or hired houses – for the summer. But the end result was that generations of British children of all social classes grew up with memories of the seaside and were keen, in their turn, to treat their own children to the same pleasures. There were few working-class organisations by the late century which did not, at some time or other, arrange excursions for members and their children to the seaside.[15]

To add to the resorts' appeal they benefited from a quasi-medical support. Dr Russell's injunction had been to *drink* seawater, but most people went to the seaside to bathe. Although this faded before other seaside attractions, there remained the fact that the resorts were thought to be much healthier than inland towns and cities. Victorians became ever more obsessed about the unhealthy state of their cities, and especially about the ailments apparently caused by the polluted atmosphere. Indeed pulmonary complaints – notably tuberculosis – were the largest of contemporary killers.[16] To escape to the fresh air, on the coast, in the countryside (later still, to mountain retreats) became a medically sanctioned antidote to the dangers of urban living. Obviously, this may have been low on the list of priorities of most seaside revellers. But it is none the less true that the resorts, many of which began to cater for the sick, the old and the convalescing, benefited from the mid- and late-Victorian debate about the nation's physical ailments and how to combat them. There were for instance few guides or brochures promoting a resort which failed to stress its health-giving or restorative qualities – normally its ozone or bracing breezes.

However, the great bulk of visitors to the coast went for other reasons. At the major resorts they could enjoy that range of newly developed commercial pleasures which, though familiar to the modern observer, were new and exciting to Victorians and Edwardians. The beaches with their stalls and shows, their donkeys and their boat trips; the piers – landmarks in the architectural development of British resorts and from which steamers plied their trade – were soon filled with entertainment booths, gadgets, machines and shows. Local and national entrepreneurs sank money into local theatres, music halls, pleasure beaches and gardens, music and band stands and spectacular buildings like Blackpool Tower. Municipal authorities similarly invested in leisure and urban provision such as sea defences, promenades, landscaped walks and gardens while also providing that core of urban regulation and control familiar to all late Victorian and Edwardian towns. There was of course enormous variation in this

10.6. Cremone Gardens,
1864

provision of leisure, depending on the size of the resort, the policy of
the city fathers and the commercial possibilities. It is tempting to think
of seaside leisure in terms of crowded piers, noisy funfairs and
boisterous and vulgar entertainments, but there was another, more
genteel, refined, rational aspect to the resorts: middle class pursuits
and enjoyments for instance, in rock pools, on cliff top walks and
assembly rooms.[17] Moreover this general picture is confused by the
fact that the resorts changed quite markedly in the years before 1914.

Changes in working-class consumer power, and changes in the

national economy which created new types of work and subgroups of relatively prosperous working people: all had an impact on leisure pursuits and upon the resorts themselves. Even the most genteel of resorts were periodically invaded by armies of people, often young men, unaccustomed to the different codes of behaviour expected of the visitor to the seaside. In fact behaviour – or misbehaviour – was a recurring theme in late Victorian and Edwardian discussion of life at the resorts.

Seaside Britain was, by the end of our period, perhaps the most spectacular example of the broader phenomenon: the emergence of modern leisure. Indeed of the ways we might choose to characterise Edwardian Britain, the story of contemporary leisure is among the most revealing. Leisure had become an enormous and varied industry in itself, with specialised employees, services and goods. It was also seen to be a social right: access to leisure, however limited (to bank holidays, trips to the coast, sports in the new elementary schools) was thought to be everyone's right. Of course it was a right severely limited and shaped by economic and social circumstance. Nonetheless, a number of late Victorian and Edwardian leisures created a code of behaviour, of play ('Playing the game', obeying the rules and playing for team rather than self) which became a moral code and a political imperative. It would be wrong, however, to think of leisure solely or even largely in terms of sports and games. Most significant perhaps was the *idea* of free time – untrammelled by work or other commitments – in which to do anything one fancied, or even to do nothing at all. This was a concept which, if commonplace today, would have been utterly alien to the early years of the nineteenth century. But it was *de rigueur*, basic, to the last years of the century. The changes between the beginning and the end of Victoria's reign were of course enormous, and are plotted elsewhere in this book. But few patterns of British behaviour provide more telling an insight into the transformation of British life than the changes in the patterns of British leisure.

Further reading

Hugh Cunningham, 'Leisure', in John Benson (ed.), *The Working Class in England, 1875–1914* (London, 1985); and *Leisure in the Industrial Revolution* (London, 1980); J.A.R. Pimlott, *The Englishman's Holiday: A Social History* (London, 1947; reprinted 1976); J.K. Walton, *The English Seaside Resort. A Social History 1750–1914* (Leicester, 1983); J.K. Walton and J. Walvin (eds), *Leisure in Britain 1780–1939* (Manchester, 1983); James Walvin, *Leisure and Society 1780–1950* (London, 1978).

The Leap in the Dark

Michael Bentley

For British citizens who are not insane or under eighteen, a good chance exists that they will be able to vote for a political party at a general election and play some part in what we usually think of as a 'democracy'. Failing to own a certain amount of property does not exclude them. Nor does failing to be male, or a member of a particular church, or the heir to some strange medieval entitlement. Yet our democracy is not merely a fragile thing but also something comparatively new. In the nineteenth century British 'democracy' passed through its most critical and interesting phase of development – from a feudal survival that had remained basically intact since 1430 towards a system of government resting on popular participation. These arrangements never threatened before our own century to become 'democratic' in the sense of every adult person's being granted the vote; but they symbolised the degree to which politicians had reacted to the new world of industrialisation and the development of social classes. Much can be learned about Victorian Britain by paying attention to what those men did and – perhaps more important – what they did not do.

We can ask some tantalising and rather hard historical questions about it all. Political parties in the 1850s and 1860s became interested in making the country 'democratic' at just the time when violent agitations in favour of a wider electorate grew *weaker*. Why? The most significant move of the country in this direction came in 1867. But why was it made then and why did a *Conservative* government embark on it? Harder still, why did a Tory administration decide to embark on reform in a more drastic and thoroughgoing spirit than the so-called Liberal government that they had just helped to throw out for proposing something more conservative? Something seems odd about a history of democracy that makes the Tory Party more revolutionary than its opponents. To make sense of it we have to find out more about who was doing the revolting. We also need to understand more than may be obvious about that peculiar mid-century Tory party. We have to decide why the future Liberal leader, Gladstone, made such a spectacular mess of the subject. We have to follow Benjamin Disraeli, the century's most astounding political tactician, through the bumps, slides and rolls that gave his direction the appearance of something like genius. We have to ask whether this 'democracy' really made much difference and, if so, to whom, as we look forward to the future with its empire and its socialists, its Chamberlains and its Pankhursts still low on the horizon.

But this is to anticipate the story; and to go forward we ought first to go back because the history of democracy emerges as a long conversation rather than a single shriek. The shriek of the French revolution of 1789 nonetheless gives a good starting point. Reports arriving from Paris gave many of Britain's politically-aware people a glimpse of what to avoid.[1] The monotonous thud of the guillotine confirmed the deeply-held belief that the ancient Greeks warning against democracy – rule by the mob – was no longer academic. Britain's ruling classes diagnosed democracy as a form of social disease and contemplated the country's catching it rather like a hypochondriac might imagine himself about to go down with 'flu.

Certainly they kept the doctor away very effectively. Even by 1870, after two major pieces of reform had extended the right to vote, or the franchise, as we call it, in 1832 and 1867, only around 2.5 million adult males in the United Kingdom had gained the right to vote out of a total population of over 30 million. Even allowing for the presence of women and children, this was hardly a handing over of the country to the whims of the people. Their reasons? Largely to keep direction of the nation's affairs in the hands of an 'aristocracy' – literally, a government by the best – who supposedly combined inbred talent and experience together with 'a stake in the country'. To merit a say in running Britain, one had to *own* a piece of it. Quite which piece one owned had become less important by 1830 than in 1750 because the cataclysm of industrialisation had produced an alternative aristocracy – a plutocracy based not on birth but on wealth: cottentots with their Lancashire mills, coal-owners with their colossal profits in Scotland, the North-East, South Wales, anonymous part-owners or directors of a canal company. Granted their power in the localities and the development of an informed public opinion through an explosive rise in newspaper readership after 1820, such people could not forever be kept outside the political system.

The Great Reform Act of 1832 brought them in.[2] To dismiss that word 'Great' simply because the increase it brought in Britain's

11.1. William Ewart Gladstone

11.2. Benjamin Disraeli, Earl of Beaconsfield

electorate turned out to be very small perhaps misses the point. A dam breached by a small hole is breached nonetheless, and the pressure it brings to bear on the remaining structure may eventually topple it altogether – the precise argument, incidentally, of those who opposed the 1832 Act. Adding half a million voters to the register, mostly by giving the vote to people occupying a house worth £10 a year, hardly amounted to a revolution. But then that tinkering had at least involved scrutinising the nation's constitution in a systematic way (for all the randomness of the result). The procedure struck some members of the British governing class as dangerously French; it compromised the picture popularised by British thinkers in the eighteenth century of a political nation that was ancient, sturdy, gnarled and haphazard, like a magnificent oak. Try as they might to present the events of 1832 as a graft on the trunk of that tree, enough had been done to call to mind a very different image.

11.3. Banquet in the Guildhall, London to celebrate the passing of the 1832 Reform Act

We also have our images looking back on the first move towards democracy, and we have to be careful in selecting among them. Very often Grey's reforming ministry appears in the textbooks as having capitulated to a middle-class threat, as having plumped for reform as the only alternative to revolution. Reading through the letters and diaries that have survived among the papers of politicians closely involved in framing the Bill of 1832 a more complicated picture emerges. Read the diarist Greville in the heady days of April 1832 and we find him writing about 'a general uncertainty': 'nobody looks upon any institution as secure, or any interest as safe'. But then glance at a letter by the Tory John Wilson Croker a couple of months before: 'Revolution progresses, and so does cholera; but so slowly that we have got accustomed to both, and no one is alarmed.'[3] Certainly when the results of the Act became clear, Croker's mood proved the more appropriate. The 'reformers' had supplemented one aristocracy with another. They had removed some, but by no means all, of the anomalies in the old system. They had introduced a few of their own.

In 1833 political observers looked around themselves and discovered a political universe quite as haywire as the one they remembered from 1831.

Indeed that 'democracy' proved a very strange environment over the next 30 years. From our vantage point it seems to have two faces: an earlier one that we associate with great popular movements like the great working-class agitation for political rights known as Chartism, or the Anti-Corn Law League's campaign to put an end to taxes on imported wheat that kept the price of bread too high or the Factory Movement with its cry for shortening the working day and improving the desperate conditions of adult and child labour. Or again we think of belly-led politics directed against the church tithe in the countryside or the terrible new Poor Law with its workhouses in the northern towns. But then there is a second phase caught in the novels not of a Dickens but rather by Trollope or the future Prime Minister, Benjamin Disraeli. Here the colours are more subdued, the contrasts less harsh. We are more aware of a world of stability and self-confidence, a sense of reform coming about, as Disraeli said in introducing his novel *Lothair* 'rather by the use of ancient forms and the restoration of the past than by political revolutions founded on abstract ideas'.[4]

Both profiles in fact conceal a good deal. Certainly an aggressive working class, envenomed by the betrayal of 1832 that had given it nothing, developed a new power in the 1830s and 1840s;[5] but the idea that it overawed governments and left them trembling for their lives is hard to find in the documents left by those supposedly distraught. Certainly the mood changed following the failure of the Chartist movement to impose its programme of political reform in 1848, but the continuities of political violence during elections and of corruption deployed on a heroic scale may be found alongside the birth of the 'respectable' craft unions and the gentleness implied in their fancy letterheads or their members' search for a terraced house in one of the better parts of town.

The continuity should come as no surprise because what suggests a new twist in the 1840s is not so much a political change as an economic one. We can make little sense of the period between 1852 and 1870 unless we visualise it against a background of economic vitality and expansion when the country's agriculture and industrial production rose to new heights: a clear contrast to the 'hungry 'forties'. Perhaps it was inevitable that the aggression of working-class politics would fade, especially among the so-called 'labour aristocracy', men whose minds were formed by the craft unions of the 1850s and 1860s and who felt keener to set themselves up as solid citizens than to act as incendiaries of unrest.[6] Political demonstrations and strikes continued, needless to say, but they took on a less threatening tone; there was a more restrained atmosphere.

One side of the reform story unfolds in the radical towns where organisations such as the Reform League and the more middle-class Reform Union directed their propaganda against Palmerston's Liberal government of 1859–65. They were helped by a groundswell of Liberal sentiment that originated in other countries: from American Northern States fighting their battle with the slave-owning South in the Civil War of 1861–4; from Italy, whose freedom-fighters greatly impressed British Liberal opinion; from Poland, whose peasants rose against their Russian tyrants; from Denmark, the victim of invasion by Bismarck's Prussia in 1864.

Now the politicians, on the other side of the fence, were not isolated from these things, and some Liberals plainly felt the impact of them. We see the process in Palmerston's Chancellor of the Exchequer, William Gladstone, as his views about democracy visibly loosen in the early 1860s until, by 1864, he is speaking about bringing the people within the pale of the constitution. But what Gladstone and other moderate Liberals had come to support by the time of Palmerston's death in 1865 reads very much like a repetition of what Grey had believed in 1832: that enough would be done both to settle agitation and strengthen the forces of stability if propertied people, and not too many of them, were allowed inside the framework where they could demonstrate the impeccable conformity that irritated those less favourably placed and support the Liberal party in a suitable vote of thanks. Besides, a sizeable group of Liberals worried about going even so far as that. The MP who would speak with the greatest passion and bitterness on the subject of reform during these years – Robert Lowe – sat on the *Liberal* side of the House.[7]

Sympathy for the people, however one defined them, was a compulsory virtue for Liberals, of course: it was part of their traditional posture as guardians of popular rights. Tories had no such problem. Even 'Conservatives', as the party of Sir Robert Peel had begun to call themselves in the 1830s, felt clear enough that '1832' must remain a final settlement. To make sense of their language after 1850, the year of Peel's death, we have to get some idea of the sheer predicament in which their former leader had left them, some hint of their desperation to recover from the disaster brought on them by Peel in 1846.

Now since the end of the war with Napoleon the farmers had been protected by legislation known to everyone as the 'Corn Laws' which gave the farmers a good price for their corn by increasing artificially the price of imported cereals. Peel had been elected in 1841 specifically to defend the rural interest by protecting the Corn Laws. So when he first undermined and then suspended them, ostensibly to help the Irish peasants whose crucial potato crop had rotted in the fields in 1845, Peel turned the Conservative Party into a spokesman for an idea without a home. It eventually found one, not in the Tory Party of Lord Derby and Disraeli but in the new Liberal Party of Lord Palmerston and Lord John Russell.

All that remained among those whose spat out Peel and his like in 1846 was a bitter taste. They had a group of people to defend, idealised in an image of solid yeomanry living an uncomplicated life of rural toil and leaving politics to those who understood them. But they had no idea what to do, apart from complaining about the end of protection and the ruin and distress that would surely follow. Yet, oddly, it did not follow. Despite the heroic efforts of Lord George Bentick and other protectionists to generate a mood of impending collapse, prosperity stubbornly increased, just as Peel had said it would. After 1852 the general economic upturn seemed to vindicate all the Peelite prophecies and gave the way for a new era of enterprise and energy. Disraeli persuaded even his Tories – the ones Peel used to call 'blockheads' – to abandon the idea of protection as party policy.[8]

That said, it is hard to see what else they could have talked about. None of the issues of the day offered the Tories any ready-made platform. Growing Liberalism abroad hardly struck Tories as something to celebrate at home. Democracy could be discussed, of course. Conservatives would need to resist it, naturally, but there again nobody looked likely to try to impose it, apart from a few radicals in the House of Commons, or perhaps Lord John Russell who had always been peculiar. They could say that the Whigs and Liberals had botched the Crimean War against the Russians in 1854–5 but then the Liberals' own supporters had already said that and done it rather better. Only Disraeli had the talent to identify lively issues and court controversy but there were times when even he appeared more of a liability than an asset. He was a baptised Jew but a Jew nonetheless: he therefore caused concern among the denser members of the Carlton Club before he said a word. His poverty was an embarrassment. The clutch of novels from the 1840s – *Coningsby, Sybil, Tancred* – had brought criticism and social jealousy as well as a modest literary reputation. Often isolated within his own party, he could do little for the moment to leaven the lump of mediocrity that surrounded him.

Besides, Disraeli lacked the strategic grip that Peel had developed through the 1830s. Peel had seen that any genuine Conservative Party would need to give itself an appeal in the towns and cities. Disraeli learned that lesson too; but he learned it largely *after* leaping in the dark towards democracy in 1867. Meanwhile he contributed to, rather than compensated for, the weak-kneed performance of the only

11.4. The Tory idealised view of a farmer

two Tory governments to take office in the twenty years after 1846. Both of them – 1852 and 1858–9 – depended on a House of Commons in which opposition parties held a majority of the seats and votes. Both radiated incompetence even when they managed to avoid total fiasco.

11.5. An election in the 1850s

The 1850s produced a chaos of parties: historians have not satisfactorily worked out who belonged to which party during a period when candidates called themselves 'Conservative', 'Liberal' or 'Liberal Conservative' almost according to whim.[9] From this period of extreme fluidity parliamentary reform emerged as an issue once more, weak and faltering at first but strong by the early 1860s. Just as in the 1820s, when pressure for extending the franchise developed during a period of party fragmentation at Westminster, so now the political parties (all of them this time) picked up the idea of cutting new figures for themselves by cutting new turf in the ground of their support. In the 1850s as in the 1820s, pressure existed in the country for widening the franchise to bring new wealth into the political system. But when the politicians at the centre thought about the question – and they seem not to have thought much about it – they couched their thoughts in the language of *opportunity* rather than of necessity. If one politician rose to his feet to proclaim the need to appease popular agitation, another would rise to ask '*What* agitation?' Bemusement often comes out of the parliamentary reports as a predominant mood, a feeling that everyone is starting to talk about parliamentary reform without feeling compelled to do so by an overwhelming public demand.

Of course this is not really so paradoxical. The very fact that the frightening Chartist agitation of the 1840s had apparently collapsed and the spokesmen of popular ambition turned into the mild-mannered men of the craft unions, supplied a more powerful argument for generosity than for niggardliness. Russell's firm announcement of 1837 that the 1832 reform would remain 'final' had then seemed appropriate in the face of widespread unrest – 'clamour out of doors', as contemporaries would have put it. But new circumstances invited new strategies; and the competition for securing the goodwill of an artisan class overrode instinctual fears of allowing England to go the way of America and degenerate into a corrupt bear-garden.

11.6. Lord John Russell

If it were done, on the other hand, better it were done *slowly*. Perhaps one day all people would become capable of voting sensibly, but for the moment the scoop must be kept shallow so as to gather only real people – those with some property, independence and integrity – and to leave behind those evocatively termed 'the residuum': persons left over when the people had been counted. The Prime Minister after 1859, Lord Palmerston, helped the process of reacting against notions of equality when he announced that democracy would simply bring the scum to the top.[10] And if colleagues like his Foreign Secretary, Earl Russell, and his Chancellor of the Exchequer, William Gladstone, took a less robust view of the prospect, they recognised that as long as their dyspeptic leader kept his grip on the House of Commons (for as a member of the Irish peerage he sat there as an MP) the horse would not escape its tight rein. Not until Palmerston's death in 1865 did those reins fall on the horse's neck with consequences that a soothsayer could have been forgiven for missing.

Everyone saw that the Liberals would struggle over a Reform Bill, just as everyone knew that they could not plausibly run away from introducing one, especially now that the arch-reformer, Earl Russell, had succeeded Lord Palmerston as Prime Minister. On his right Russell faced a powerful landowning interest in the section of the party still called 'Whig'. These men frequently expressed an eighteenth-century terror of the mob and included among their number a collection of rabid opponents of democracy whom John Bright liked to call the Cave of Adullam after the place to which David fled from Saul, 'and everyone that was discontented, gathered themselves unto him'.[11] On his left, meanwhile, stood the radicals who would obviously desert him at once if he listened to the cries from the Cave and chose the path of timidity. Gladstone, who played a considerable role in framing the Liberal Bill, found government a more complicated place than it had seemed under Palmerston. The man who had spoken two years before about bringing the people within the pale of the constitution decided now to leave most of them beyond it.

11.7. *The Political Tailors*, a *Punch* cartoon of 1867, satirising the political machinations of Gladstone and Disraeli

PUNCH, OR THE LONDON CHARIVARI.—May 11, 1867.

THE POLITICAL TAILORS.

Dizzy. "NOW, THEN, GLADSTONE, JUMP UP!—YOU PROMISED TO LEND A HELPING HAND, YOU KNOW

Gladstone. "NO, I'M 'ON STRIKE,' AND YOU MAY FINISH THE JOB AS YOU BEST CAN."

Calculations had turned on avoiding what was called working class 'preponderance'. But since about a quarter of those people believed by contemporaries to fall within that category already seemed to have acquired the vote during the prosperity that had unquestionably arrived during the 1850s, the only way to secure the future lay in producing a reform proposal that hardly seemed worth the breath. The Liberals brought forth a mouse. The Bill went down in the Commons before a contemptuous amendment; the government resigned in disgrace; Gladstone could find no cave deep enough to hide his humiliation.

So much might perhaps have been foreseen, granted the divisions within the party and its history of internal warfare. But no one could have predicted the use that Disraeli would make of the opportunity. The new Conservative government would have no majority: it was hard to see what it could realistically attempt. It could survive only as long as the Liberals hated one another more than the government. But Disraeli, at the Exchequer as Gladstone had been, digested this fact more thoroughly than anyone on either bench and began enthusiastically and remorselessly the task of making the Liberals more miserable with one another than ever. What even he did not yet appreciate was how far he was willing to go. Lord Derby coined the phrase 'a leap in the dark' to describe what happened over the next few months, but it was Disraeli who made the Tories jump.

Conservatives dislike jumping and they would need more than a little persuasion, even in the circumstances of 1867, to do something uncharacteristic. And indeed at first Disraeli permitted the groaners and growlers around him to press him towards caution. There would have to be a Reform Bill of some kind, but surely they could postpone it for a year or two. But when Disraeli made noises of this kind in the House of Commons, their sole result was to give comfort to the Liberals, and a comfortable Liberal party could mean only one thing for the government – its death. So Disraeli gave the accelerator a stab.

He would bring in, he said, not just vague resolutions but a *Bill*. More groans and growls surrounded him, not merely from the Cave but from his own cabinet colleagues, and reasonably so since Disraeli had not done them the courtesy of asking their opinion. He listened to them just once more. In deference to the requests of his laggards for caution he brought before the House in February 1867 a Bill of studied defensiveness. Immediately he found that his own back-benchers disliked it; they disliked it, not because they wanted to lunge towards democracy, but because they wanted the party to take whatever measures were necessary to save them from Gladstone. Better democracy than Gladstone, as it were. Better to risk a radical departure that would leave Gladstone down the hole he was in than to risk giving him the opportunity for parliamentary victories such as the one he achieved over this abortive Bill. Better to chance their arm in a more popular electoral system than to slope off back to the wilderness of opposition in which they had been languishing for the past 20 years. But that meant that the Tory proposal would need to be truly appalling: something so 'liberal' that Gladstone would not be able to oppose it without contradicting everything he had himself said during the previous session; something, in fact, that would encourage the radicals to mistake Disraeli for their mother.

Caution had brought Disraeli to the very edge of defeat. Cowardice had turned out to be more dangerous than courage. He reverted to his original plan of going for a Bill that would enfranchise considerable numbers of town-dwellers; he would fly the kite that the Conservative Party was prepared to give the vote to the urban householder. He knew perfectly well that three of his growlers would resign on the spot and since two of them, Lords Cranborne and Carnarvon, were not lightweights, the decision demanded a certain coolness. Once taken, moreover, it could not be untaken. Not only would the party need to commit itself to a substantially larger electorate, but it would be obliged also to back a Bill which the government (a crucial point, this, in the entire episode) would have no hope of controlling during its passage through the House of Commons because it had no majority there. When the radicals began to throw their amendments at the Bill, as they surely would in order to increase the range of its provisions and thereby the size of the electorate, the government would have to bite the bullet and accept them. When Gladstone suggested anything at all – sensible or silly, controversial or uncontentious – he would have to be squashed in order to deepen his own party's disgust at his ineffectuality.

Disraeli carried out both operations with a mastery of parliamentary atmosphere perhaps unparalleled.[12] Through that congested session during the spring and summer of 1867, the government accepted so many revisions of the original proposal that the number of people to whom the Bill now threatened to give the vote actually trebled. Gladstone meanwhile sank without trace. A parliamentary commentator overheard two Tory MPs chatting in the lobby in June. '"Gladstone is done for", chuckles one Conservative to another, who replies with a laugh and a shrug!'

These events obviously provoked enormous popular interest and indeed participation. For while all this drama had preoccupied most politicians at Westminster, democracy had already been speaking for itself within walking distance of the House of Commons in Hyde Park. The Reform League had got up a massive demonstration in May in favour of greater democracy. Despite the meeting's having been banned by the tearful Home Secretary, Spencer Walpole, it had gone ahead regardless and staged an impressive display of popular enthusiasm, though there had been no significant violence. There are two schools of thought among historians about the importance of the demonstration. One group sees in this meeting and a previous one in

1866 a major cause of the government deciding to rush towards reform out of a fear of revolutionary consequences if it had not.[13] The other view, which seems in general more persuasive, sees these meetings as important events in providing a framework and context for a story whose origins and driving forces nevertheless lay elsewhere. But whichever way one reads it, the summer of 1867 plainly became a toboggan ride whose speed and direction had largely now escaped Disraeli's control.

Inevitably the effects of Disraeli's Reform Act went beyond what had been envisaged at the outset. Not that the figures overall seem startling. Taken as a whole, the electorate of the United Kingdom rose by only some 80 per cent to just under 2.5 million. But that includes Ireland, where the changes made in 1867 were very modest, except in Belfast. It includes Scotland but fails to reveal how great the difference turned out to be in the Scottish boroughs where an increase of nearly 180 per cent took place. In England and Wales this global total bunches together the borough seats, whose electorates changed dramatically in some places, and the county ones where they did not until 1884. The real bite came in particular localities: in a great city like Birmingham, for example, where the electorate leapt from 8000 to 43,000. Northern industrial towns like Huddersfield became centres of voting power for the first time. And in what came to be called the 'Celtic Fringe', places like Merthyr Tydfil in South Wales or Dundee in eastern Scotland received enormous boosts to their electoral importance.[14]

Yet ultimately it came to more than a question of figures. The Disraeli government had redrawn the political map of Britain and by doing so had rewritten agendas for all political parties. The beginnings of the power of an industrial employer class and confrontation with a young trade union organisation – the TUC dates from 1868 – are obvious in the years that follow Disraeli's leap and they gather pace from that impetus. A distinctive form of Labour Party would not appear until 1893, but the Reform Act had inadvertently prepared its soil in important ways. For the classes at which reform had directly been targeted, the artisans and the lower middle class, a way had to be found to cement links and sustain support. It is no accident that we see the Conservative Party trying through the early 1870s to tame the tiger whose tail it now held by forming organisations in the towns, by providing working men's clubs in which politics could take second place to cheap beer and by turning the mind of Britain away from class friction at home to the great example of 'harmony' abroad: the British empire with India its jewel and Victoria its empress.

One can, of course, overargue the case. When the novelist Anthony Trollope fought and lost Beverley in East Yorkshire in the first general election after the Reform Act, he had the satisfaction of watching the place disfranchised for its gross electoral corruption. His experience reminds us that when we stand at 1870 and look forwards, democracy as we think of it has certainly not come into view. Not only is corruption still rife, but a very substantial slice of the working class still has no vote in parliamentary elections. Nor have *all* women: they would remain without the vote until 1918, though we ought to remember that they did gain some foothold in local elections from 1869.[15] Yet when all the qualifications have been made and the lack of revolution conceded, something important and instructive had taken place in 1867 and it leaves an echo with us a century later. It provided a threshold across which British politics begin in retrospect to appear recognisably 'modern'. The fascination of the story lies in the degree to which it emerged from a style of parliamentary manoeuvre that an eighteenth-century political manager — Robert Walpole or a William Pitt — might have understood and admired.

Further reading

Walter Bagehot, *The English Constitution* (London, 1867); Michael Bentley, *Politics Without Democracy 1815–1914: perception and preoccupation in British government* (Harmondsworth, 1984); Robert Blake, *Disraeli* (1966); Maurice Cowling, *1867: Disraeli, Gladstone and Revolution* (Cambridge, 1967); *Essays on Reform* (London, 1867); F.B. Smith, *The Making of the Second Reform Bill* (Cambridge, 1966).

CHAPTER TWELVE

The Invention of the Past

Peter J. Bowler

The Victorians were fascinated by the past. They read historical novels, and even the works of academic historians, with an enthusiasm that betrays a deep concern for the origins of their own society. They were equally excited by the extension of history into new areas. In the course of the nineteenth century, archaeologists created the study of prehistory, while geologists used the fossil record to reconstruct the history of life on the earth and to ask questions about the origin of the human race. But this fascination with the past had a definite purpose. The Victorians became convinced that history represents a progressive development toward their own civilisation as the pinnacle of human achievement. They did not merely discover – they *invented* the past, creating an image of history that would help them to explain and to feel comfortable with what was going on in the present.

Why did this interest in the past emerge during the nineteenth century? The simplest answer is that people became aware of the fact that they were living in an ever-changing world. There had always been social change, of course, but it had usually taken place so slowly that no one had noticed. Throughout this book we have seen how the pace of change began to quicken in the decades around 1800. The French Revolution and the Napoleonic Wars helped to create a sense that the old order of European society was being swept away. More immediately, the social reorganisation that accompanied the Industrial Revolution began to have an increasing effect on everyday life. For the first time, people realised that they were living under conditions which differed significantly from the way their parents had lived – and they hoped that their children's lives would be different yet again. A changing world can be frightening, however, unless one feels able to understand the process of change and to see where it is leading.

History was one way of seeking reassurance. By studying past changes in their society, the Victorians hoped to understand how the present state of affairs had originated and how things might develop in the future. All too often, though, their hopes and fears about the future helped to influence their interpretation of the past.

History had been popular in the eighteenth century, as the success of Edward Gibbon's *Decline and Fall of the Roman Empire* reveals. But studying the rise and fall of ancient civilisations does not necessarily generate a sense of *cumulative* change in history. By the early nineteenth century, the Romantic movement had helped to create an idealised image of past epochs, often glorifying the more rugged or primitive aspects of our ancestors' lives. Everyone was now in a position to appreciate this sense of how the past differed from the present. Popular novels such as Sir Walter Scott's *Ivanhoe* helped to create a picture of medieval chivalry as the foundation upon which a later refinement of manners would be built. Later on, Charles Kingsley's *Westward Ho*! portrayed the adventurous Elizabethans as pioneers of the spirit that was building the British empire.

British historians tended to assume that their country had been particularly fortunate in its social development. From Magna Carta through to the Glorious Revolution and beyond, Britain was supposed to have led the way toward the creation of a society based on individual freedom. Constitutional history thus became a means of defining those aspects of nineteenth-century life upon which the British most prided themselves. This was most apparent in the work of Thomas Babbington Macaulay, whose *History of England* appeared between 1849 and 1861. Historians such as Macaulay were so anxious to celebrate the superiority of British institutions that they were soon accused of writing 'Whig history'. The Whigs were the ancestors of the Liberal Party, and Whig history was history rewritten to enhance the role played by the political values of this party. The term 'Whig history' has since come to mean almost any attempt to represent the past as a simple progression toward the modern state of affairs.[1] Among historians it has become a term of abuse, because it implies that the interpretation of the past has been deliberately distorted by the demands of the present. The Victorians' image of the past *was* often biased in this way, yet we should not forget that any history (including the history in this book) is an interpretation of the past and will thus tend to reflect the interests of those who do the interpreting.

In its original form, Whig history treated Britain as a unique focus of social progress – as defined by the standards of the rising middle class. But the growing optimism of European culture also generated a far more pervasive sense that history records the inexorable progress of civilisation. The idea of progress had first been emphasised by radical writers such as William Godwin at the end of the eighteenth century.[2] They tried to justify their calls for future reforms by suggesting that such improvements were an inevitable continuation of a long-standing historical trend. Starting from the earliest, most primitive state of society, history revealed a gradual – if irregular – development toward higher levels of civilisation. The most influential social philosopher of the nineteenth century, Herbert Spencer, certainly believed that *laissez-faire* capitalism was the highest form of society, but he also held that it was the natural end-produce of a vast process of social evolution. Spencer, whose first book of social issues appears in 1851, devised a 'Synthetic Philosophy' which was both a system of morality and a sociological theory based on the notion of historical development.[3] He was interested not so much in the uniquely progressive environment of Britain, but in what he regarded as the universal trend toward the British kind of society.

The Victorians were so confident of their own superiority that they inevitably saw other societies as being at a 'lower' stage of development than their own. The expansion of European power around the globe had revealed a bewildering variety of cultures with

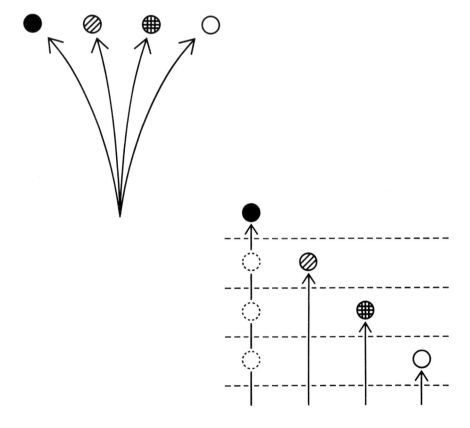

12.1. Two models of cultural evolution. The diagram on the left illustrates a branching model of evolution, in which all of the end-products are of equal status, and none can be treated as the goal toward which all evolution is tending. The diagram on the right corresponds to Tylor's model of cultural evolution as a progression in which all lines advance through the same hierarchy of developmental stages. Here all lines are moving toward the same goal, and those which have progressed more slowly will have reached stages equivalent to earlier points in the history of the most advanced varying degrees of technological sophistication. The founders of the new science of cultural anthropology wanted to understand how the human race could exhibit such a wide range of customs and social structures. The work of Edward B. Taylor, whose *Researches on the Early History of Mankind* appeared in 1865, is typical of how the Victorian anthropologists tackled the problem.[4] Modern anthropologists accept that each society represents an equally valid expression of mankind's cultural potential. In effect, they use a branching model of cultural evolution, in which each culture can be seen as an independent line of development. But Tylor and his fellow Victorians could not accept such a model, because they were convinced that their own culture represented the high point of human achievement, and was thus the goal toward which all other societies must be developing. Instead, they adopted a model of cultural evolution based on a linear progression through a fixed hierarchy of stages. All societies were imagined to be advancing in parallel along the same scale of development, but they were advancing at different rates, so in the modern world they have reached different levels of social development. European civilisation was, of course, supposed to have reached the highest level, while other societies have lagged behind in the ascent of the scale, perhaps because they have developed in less stimulating environments. On this model, all social evolution has the same goal, and the 'lower' societies in the world today illustrate what the Europeans' own ancestors must have looked like at earlier stages in their progress along the scale. As the title of Tylor's book illustrates, the study of modern 'primitive' cultures was supposed to throw light on 'the early history of mankind'. The geographical diversity of mankind was thus explained in historical terms by means of the idea of progress.

Because industrial progress was the symbol of European success, the Victorians ranked other societies by their level of technological achievement. A low level of industrial development was taken as an automatic sign of a 'primitive' culture. Some of the most technologically unsophisticated societies – including the Australian aborigines – were known to be still using stone tools. Tylor was well aware that archaeologists had now confirmed that the earliest inhabitants of Europe had also made tools of stone. Scandinavian archaeologists had introduced the 'Three Age' system to describe the development of toolmaking skills in Europe.[5] The ages of stone, bronze and iron showed that a progression could be traced out in prehistory, long before written records became available. The anthropologists saw technologically primitive peoples such as the Australian aborigines as relics of mankind's original stone-age culture, preserved through into the present in areas isolated from the general march of progress. These peoples were living illustrations of the long-surpassed ancestral stages of European culture that the archaeologists had revealed.

Archaeology extended the idea of progress back into the more distant past, but raised potentially controversial issues. Traditionally, it had been assumed that the human race appeared on the earth only a few thousand years ago, so that the Old Testament gave a complete record of our early spiritual development. But archaeologists were now discovering very primitive stone tools alongside the bones of extinct animals, in deposits that the geologists assured them were tens, if not hundreds of thousands of years old. Many were reluctant to accept the implications of these discoveries, but around 1860 geologists such as Charles Lyell began to advocate the vast antiquity of the human race.[6] The study of prehistory was thus extended into a new area – and immediately interpreted in terms of progress. In his *Prehistoric Times* of 1865, John Lubbock coined the terms 'neolithic' and 'palaeolithic' to denote the new and the old stone ages, the old by definition relating to the most primitive stone tools. The Three Age system could thus be expanded, and by 1870 archaeologists had already begun to subdivide the palaeolithic into a sequence of cultures named after characteristic French sites (see Figure 12.2).[7] These stone-age cultures were seen as a universal progressive sequence through which all European peoples had advanced with little geographical variation. As in Tylor's sytem of cultural development, the assumption was that throughout the vast period in which mankind had inhabited the earth, culture had steadily progressed toward higher levels of industrial development.

The geologists who helped to extend human antiquity were already familiar with the idea that the earth itself has a history stretching back far beyond even the earliest origin of mankind. In the seventeenth century, Archbishop James Ussher had worked out that the earth and the human race had been created together in 4004 BC, exactly as described in the Book of Genesis. By 1800, this view of the earth's origin had crumbled in the face of a major scientific revolution leading to the establishment of modern geology. The geologists of the early nineteenth century established the relative sequence in which the various types of rock had been formed. They were sure that a vast period of time had passed during which the rocks of the earth's crust had been laid down, folded into mountains, and eroded – all before the human race had appeared on the scene.[8] The fossils entombed in the rocks revealed that the present population of animals was not the first to inhabit the earth, but merely the last in a long sequence of creations. In effect, the geologists opened up a whole new area of history. It could be argued that only a society that was becoming accustomed to rapid change could have contemplated the possibility

12.2. New classifications for prehistory. This table illustrates how the Three Age system of prehistory was extended by mid-nineteenth-century archaeologists. The stone age was first divided into the neolithic and palaeolithic, and the palaeolithic then subdivided into a sequence of cultures named after characteristic French sites

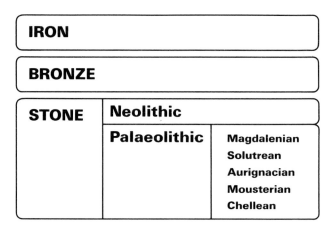

that the earth itself is impermanent. Potentially, the discovery of the earth's past could threaten the traditional view that mankind plays a central role in God's creation. Yet we shall see that the geologists were able to retain a sense of purpose in the history of life on the earth by extending the idea of progress to the whole animal kingdom.

The discovery of extinct animals attracted wide attention. In 1821, William Buckland explored a cave at Kirkdale in Yorkshire, where the bones of animals no longer found in Europe were buried beneath a thick layer of mud. He showed that the cave had been a hyenas' den, which he assumed to have been buried in the mud created by Noah's flood.[9] Yet Buckland knew that this catastrophe was merely the last in a long sequence of geological events not recorded by the Bible. Later on he accepted that the evidence could best be explained by postulating not a flood but an ice age in the recent geological past, immediately preceding the emergence of modern conditions. The earth itself seemed to have experienced revolutions as traumatic as any in human history.

Long before hyenas had roamed the Yorkshire dales, the fossil record revealed a period in which reptiles had been the dominant form of life.[10] From Lyme Regis in Dorset came the remains of the plesiosaur, a strange aquatic reptile. But the most spectacular inhabitants of the 'Age of Reptiles' were the dinosaurs. It was Buckland who described the first known dinosaur in 1823, a giant carnivore which he named *Megalosaurus*. It had been found at Stonesfield in Oxfordshire. Another equally spectacular discovery from Sussex was described in the following year – a large herbivorous dinosaur named *Iguanodon*, whose fossilised teeth were found in a pile of stones intended for roadmending. It was the anatomist Richard Owen who coined the name 'dinosaur' in 1841 to include all these 'terribly great lizards'. Later on, Owen constructed life-sized models of *Megalosaurus* and *Iguanodon* in the grounds to which the Crystal Palace was moved after the Great Exhibition of 1851. They are still there today, rather inaccurate by modern standards, but spectacular nonetheless.

The Victorians were fascinated by this evidence of primeval life. Buckland's lectures at Oxford were immensely popular. Books on geology and palaeontology sold as well as novels. At the beginning of *Bleak House*, when Dickens wanted to evoke the sense of alienation created by the fog and mud of a London winter, he wrote that 'it

12.3. The Megalosaurus, Crystal Palace

would not be wonderful to meet a Megalosaurus, forty feet long or so, waddling like an elephantine lizard up Holborn hill'.[11] Museums were built to house the spectacular new discoveries, culminating with the Natural History Museum, designed by Owen in the 1860s but not built until 1881. A statue of Owen now stands at the head of the Museum's main staircase – with his great rivals, Darwin and Huxley, confined to a room beneath his feet.

12.4. William Buckland lecturing in Oxford

But what did this succession of fossil populations mean? Did the revolutions in the history of life indicate only a haphazard chaos of creation and extinction? If so, the traditional view that the universe was created by a wise and benevolent God would be undermined. Some Victorians certainly foresaw this possibility, as when Tennyson wrote in his *In Memoriam* of 'Nature, red in tooth and claw'.[12] In this pessimistic mood, Tennyson saw nature as totally indifferent to the life of the individual or the species. Yet the majority of Victorians drew back from this precipice of unbelief. They could tolerate the thought of a changing world only if it were supposed to change in a purposeful direction. They found a solution to their dilemma by applying the idea of progress to the fossil record.

The general outline of the fossil record certainly seemed to indicate a progressive development of life on the earth. The earliest fossils were primitive invertebrates, Trilobites, from the Cambrian rocks of Wales. Next came the strange armoured fish of the Devonian era, best seen in the Old Red Sandstone of Scotland. They were followed by the Age of Reptiles, which had been popularised by the discovery of the dinosaurs. Finally mammals appeared, first as strange primitive forms, and then running through to more recently extinct forms such as the woolly mammoth and Buckland's hyenas. The human race had only appeared since the last geological revolution. Life had clearly progressed along the chain of being toward the high point of creation: ourselves.[13]

The belief that life had progressed toward mankind became popular before the theory of evolution. At first, it was simply assumed that God had created the succession of ever-higher forms. But the Victorians were convinced that human progress occurred as a result of human activity – not through divine miracles – and it is hardly surprising that they soon began to suspect that the development of life might also be the result of a natural process. What we now call the theory of evolution became the subject of popular discussion some time before Darwin's *Origin of Species* appeared. As early as 1844, the Edinburgh writer Robert Chambers published an anonymous book called *Vestiges of the Natural History of Creation*. It argued that the divine plan of creation unfolded naturally toward its goal, without the need for repeated miracles, and used the fossil record to illustrate the ascent of life. Chambers' book was controversial because he quite explicitly discussed the possibility that the human race was the product of a development within the animal kingdom.[14] If mankind was to become part of nature – no longer raised above it by the possession of an immortal soul – nature itself would have to be seen as a purposeful system if human life was to retain a purpose.

The publication of the *Origin of Species* in 1859 was important because it turned the idea of evolution from a popular debating point into a respected scientific theory.[15] To do this, however, Darwin had to go against the trend that saw all development as a necessary progression toward a higher state. Darwin was not interested in the ascent of life revealed by the fossil record – indeed, he held that the fossils provide very poor evidence for evolution. He had been drawn to the subject by his studies of the geographical distribution of species, while on a voyage around the world aboard the survey ship *HMS Beagle*. Darwin's theory of natural selection was an attempt to explain how a species adapts to changes in its local environment. If members of a single original species migrate to a number of different locations, each group would adapt in its own way, and the single original species would split into several later ones. The *Origin of Species* contains a diagram showing that in Darwin's view, evolution has to be seen *not* as the ascent of a ladder toward a final goal, but as a branching tree, with each branch moving off in its own independent direction. In such a theory it was impossible to treat the human race as the goal of the whole evolutionary process.

The theory of natural selection depended on the random variation among the individuals of a population. Some individuals would by chance be better adapted to a new environment, and would do well in the struggle for existence caused by the tendency of the population to breed beyond its food supply. In Darwin's theory, the 'survival of the fittest' meant only that those best adapted to the local environment would survive and breed, thus enhancing their characters in the next generation. There was no implication that the 'fittest' would be better in any absolute sense that would guarantee the progress of life toward higher states. Because Darwin denied the purposeful character of evolution, many of his contemporaries refused to accept his theory of natural selection. They praised Darwin for demonstrating the fact of evolution, but ignored or misrepresented his explanation of how it worked. Popular evolutionary texts of the 1870s frequently restructured the 'tree of life' so that it had a main 'trunk', all other developments being mere side-branches. There was still a central theme in the history of life, leading to the appearance of ever-higher levels of

12.5. *HMS Beagle*

intelligence and culminating in mankind. The progress of civilisation could be seen as an inevitable continuation of the upward trend that had led to the evolution of the human species.

But what of 'social Darwinism'?[6] The Victorians certainly applied Darwinian terms such as the 'struggle for existence' and the 'survival of the fittest' to social evolution but they did so in a way that violated the basic principles of Darwin's theory. It was Herbert Spencer, not Darwin, who coined the term 'survival of the fittest', yet Spencer was never an enthusiastic Darwinian and later attacked those scientists who regarded natural selection as the sole mechanism of evolution. Spencer certainly drew an analogy between biological and social evolution, but he saw the struggle for existence in a free-enterprise society as a stimulus that would encourage everyone in the race for self-improvement. The principle of encouraging *Self Help* (the title of a popular book by Samuel Smiles published in the same year as the *Origin of Species*) expressed what the Victorians really hoped to gain from the free-enterprise system. Everyone would be given the freedom to get on in life, and those who contributed most to social and economic progress would be rewarded by personal success. Failure to contribute would be punished by the suffering of economic hardship – but most people would respond to this stimulus in a positive way, rather than allowing themselves to be eliminated by starvation. The Victorians wanted a theory of evolution in which individual enterprise and initiative were the driving forces. But they also wanted to believe that progress was inevitable because success would depend on creative activity, not on mere ruthlessness and brute cunning. They could thus adopt Darwinian language, while ignoring the fact that Darwin's theory challenged the whole idea of progress.

When applied to the origins of the human race, this modified interpretation of Darwin's theory seemed to fit in quite naturally with Tylor's view of cultural progress. The anthropologists saw 'lower' – that is, technologically unsophisticated – cultures as relics of earlier stages in the advance toward modern civilisation. But now those races which had preserved the primitive levels of culture could be seen as *biological* relics of earlier stages in the process by which the human species had advanced from the ancestral ape. White anthropologists had already tried to show that black races had certain ape-like characters, and now the theory of evolution seemed to show why this should be so.[17] Trapped in areas with a less stimulating environment, these races had fallen behind in the ascent from the apes. They had thus retained ape-like features, a lower level of intelligence and, of course, a more primitive level of culture. This apparently neat link between biological and social progress satisfied the Victorians' sense of their own racial and cultural superiority. The 'lower' races could be dismissed as the losers in nature's great race toward perfection. Their eventual enslavement or extermination by the triumphant whites would follow as a direct application of the principle of the 'survival of the fittest'. This crude synthesis of the Darwinian emphasis on struggle with a distinctly pre-Darwinian model of progressive evolution would serve as a perfect justification for late-ninteenth century imperialism.

12.6. The empire at work

The nineteenth century saw the extension of the study of history into entirely new areas, and the deliberate construction of an image of the past based on the idea of progress. The history of life on the earth, the origin of the human species, and the development of civilisation, were all seen as parts of a continuous progressive trend leading toward the present state of affairs. Progress in the past encouraged the hope that the future would yield further development. Yet this model was also used as a means of dismissing other societies and races as 'primitives' left behind in the advance and doomed to failure in the modern world. There was an element of narrow-mindedness and intolerance lying behind the self-confident facade of Victorian thought. In the twentieth century, anthropologists have realised that the diversity of the human species is so great that the races and cultures cannot be arranged into a simple evolutionary hierarchy. Yet the continued prevalence of racist attitudes in our society suggests that even today, there are many who have not yet abandoned the Victorians' image of the past.

Further reading

P.J. Bowler, *Evolution: the History of an Idea* (Berkeley, Los Angeles and London, 1984); J.W. Burrow, *Evolution and Society: a Study in Victorian Social Theory* (Cambridge, 1966); G. Daniel, *A Hundred and Fifty Years of Archaeology* (London, 1975); M. Mandelbaum, *History, Man and Reason: a Study in Nineteenth-Century Thought* (Baltimore and London, 1971); M.J.S. Rudwick, *The Meaning of Fossils: Episodes in the History of Paleontology* (New York, 1976): M. Ruse, *The Darwinian Revolution: Science Red in Tooth and Claw* (Chicago and London, 1979).

Notes

1. The Echo of the Tumbril *Michael Broers*

1. These figures are drawn from I.R. Christie, *Wars and Revolutions, 1760–1815* (London 1982), p. 158.
2. Edmund Burke, *Reflections on the Revolution in France* (Harmondsworth, 1969), p. 130 (first published 1790).
3. Cited in C. Emsley, *British Society and the French Wars, 1793–1815* (London, 1979), p. 22.
4. C. Webster, *The Foreign Policy of Castlereagh, 1812–15* (London, 1931), p. 7.
5. The glorification of the Terror by the French Left was begun by A. Mathiez with *Girondins et Montagnards* (1930) and has been perpetuated by his Marxist disciples, notably in the works of the late A. Soboul. For English readers, the most vivid and memorable anti-Jacobin account of the Terror is still Carlyle's *The French Revolution*, 2 vols (London, 1837), while the tradition in France is best seen in Michelet's *La Revolution Française* (Paris, 1847–53).
6. Cited in Emsley, *British Society*, p. 117.
7. M. Elliott, *Partners in Revolution: France and the United Irishmen* (New Haven and London, 1984); R. Wells, *Insurrection, the British Experience, 1795–1803* (Gloucester, 1983); E.P. Thompson, *The Making of the English Working Class* (Harmondsworth, 1963).
8. Emsley, *British Society*, p. 16. For the complexities and political variety within the Loyalist Associations, see: D.E. Ginter, 'The Loyalist Association Movement of 1792–93 and British public opinion,' *Historical Journal*, IX (Cambridge, 1966).
9. *The Anti-Jacobin*, no. 1, 20 Nov., 1797, cited in Emsley, *British Society*, p. 65.
10. See F.K. Prochaska, 'English state trials in the 1790s: a case study', *Journal of British Studies*, XIII (1973).
11. R. Wells, *Insurrection, the British Experience* 1795-1803 (Gloucester, 1983), Chapter 5, 'The Naval Mutinies of 1797'.

2. A Question of Machinery *Maxine Berg*

1. E.J. Hobsbawm, *Industry and Empire* (London, 1968), p. 63.
2. Thomas Carlyle, cited in Raymond Williams, *The Long Revolution* (Harmondsworth, 1965), p. 88, and *James Nasmyth, An Autobiography*, Samuel Smiths (1883), cited in Humphrey Jennings, *Pandemonium. The Coming of the Machine as Seen by Contemporary Observers, 1660–1886* (London, 1985).
3. E.A. Wrigley, 'The growth of population in eighteenth century England: a conundrum resolved', *Past and Present*, XCVIII *(1983)*.
4. *See N.F.R. Crafts, British Economic Growth during the Industrial Revolution (Oxford, 1985).*
5. Ibid.
6. Wrigley, 'The growth of population', p. 122.
7. Thomas Bewick, cited in Roy Porter, *English Society in the Eighteenth Century* (Harmondsworth, 1982), p. 228; Arthur Young (General Report on Enclosures, 1808), cited in Porter, *English Society*, p. 229. See Keith Snell, *Annals of the Labouring Poor* (Cambridge, 1985), pp. 339–43.
8. E.A. Wrigley, 'Urban growth and agricultural change: England and the Continent in the early modern period', *J. Interdisciplinary History*, XX, 4(Spring 1985), 686, and D.E.C. Eversley 'Industry and Trade, 1500–1800', in the *Victoria County History of Warwickshire*, vol. 7 (1964).
9. Adam Smith, *An Enquiry into the Nature and Causes of the Wealth of Nations*, (1776), Book IV, Chapter viii (Oxford, 1976), p. 644; Adrian Randall, 'Labour and the Industrial Revolution in the West of England woollen industry', University of Birmingham PhD Thesis (1979), pp. 249–54. Cited in Maxine Berg, *The Age of Manufactures, Industry, Innovation and Work in Britain 1700–1820* (London, 1985), p. 157.
10. Josiah Tucker (1757) cited in Porter, *English Society*, pp. 213–14. Cited in Dorothy George, *England in Transition, Life and Work in the Eighteenth Century* (London, 1931), p. 133 and Ivy Pinchbeck and Margaret Hewitt, *Children in English Society*, vol. II (London, 1973), pp. 395–6.
11. Cited in David Vincent, *Bread, Knowledge and Freedom, A Study of Nineteenth Century Working Class Autobiography* (London, 1981), p. 76 and T.C. Smout, *A History of the Scottish People, 1560–1830* (London, 1969), p. 399.
12. See Berg, *The Age of Manufactures*, pp. 147–8.
13. Samuel Bamford, *The Autobiography of Samuel Bamford*, vol. I. *Early Days* (1848–9) (London, 1967), p. 208.
14. Pat Hudson, 'Proto-industrialisation: the case of the West Riding wool textile industry in the 18th and 19th centuries', *History Workshop Journal*, 12 (1981) and 'From manor to mill: the West Riding in transition', in M. Berg, P. Hudson and M. Sonenscher, *Manufacture in Town and County before the Factory* (Cambridge, 1983).

15. Julia de Lacey Mann, *The Cloth Industry in the West of England from 1640–1880* (Oxford 1971), p. 114 and Herbert Heaton, *The Yorkshire Woollen Industry*, 2nd edn (Oxford, 1965), p. 419; John Styles 'Embezzlement in industry and the law in England 1500–1800', in Berg, Hudson and Sonenscher, *Manufacture in Town and County*, p. 178.

16. I owe the story of Gabriel Jars to J.R. Harris. T.S. Ashton, *An Eighteenth Century Industrialist, Peter Stubs of Warrington 1756–1806* (Manchester, 1939), p. 36.

17. Heaton, *Yorkshire Woollen and Worsted Industry*, p. 354.

18. Bamford, *Early Days*, p. 304.

19. William Reddy, *The Rise of Market Culture* (Cambridge, 1985).

20. Cited in Vincent, *Bread, Knowledge and Freedom*, p. 69.

3. From Retribution to Reform *Boyd Hilton*

1. W.E. Gladstone to his wife, 12 Oct. 1845, *Correspondence on Church and Religion of William Ewart Gladstone*, ed. D.C. Lathbury (London, 1910), II, p. 266.

2. Graham to Peel, 18 Oct. 1845, Peel Papers, British Library Add. MSS., 40451, ff.400–1.

3. *Memoirs by Sir Robert Peel*, ed. Earl Stanhope and Edward Cardwell (London, 1857), II, p. 125.

4. Perceval in House of Commons, 20 Mar. 1832, *Hansard's Parliamentary Debates*, 3rd series XI, pp. 577–81.

5. J.R. McCulloch, *Considerations on Partnerships with Limited Liability* (London, 1856), pp. 10–11.

6. Charlotte Williams-Wynn to Maurice, Apr. 1858, *Memorials of Charlotte Williams-Wynn*, ed. her sister (London, 1877), pp. 246–7.

4. The New Babylons *Penelope J. Corfield*

1. W. Hutton, *The Life of William Hutton*, ed. C. Hutton (1816), p. 41.

2. Contrast W. Hutton, *An History of Birmingham* (1783; reprinted 1976), p. 23, and Mrs Elton in Jane Austen, *Emma* (1816; Harmondsworth, 1969), p. 310. And for modern historians' interpretations, see variously C. Gill, *History of Birmingham, Vol. I: Manor and Borough to 1865* (Oxford, 1952), and J. Money, *Experience and Identity: Birmingham and the West Midlands, 1760–1800* (Manchester, 1977).

3. Consult S. Shesgreen (ed.), *Engravings by Hogarth: 101 Prints* (New York, 1973); F. Antal, *Hogarth and his Place in European Art* (New York, 1962); and R. Paulson, *Hogarth: His Life, Art, and Times* (New Haven, Mass. 1971), 2 vols.

4. M. Falkus, 'Lighting in the Dark Ages of English economic history: town streets before the Industrial Revolution' in D.C. Coleman and A.H. John (eds), *Trade, Government and Economy in Pre-Industrial England* (London, 1976), pp. 248–73.

5. Oliver Goldsmith, *She Stoops to Conquer: Or, the Mistakes of a Night* (1773): Act, 1 scene 1.

6. Sidney Smith, *Selected Letters*, ed. N.C. Smith (Oxford, 1981), p. 170.

7. T. Smollett, *The Expedition of Humphry Clinker* (1771; new edn 1831), p. 41. For highly contrasting approaches to the history of Bath, see A. Barbeau, *Life and Letters at Bath in the Eighteenth Century* (London, 1904) and R.S. Neale, *Bath: A Social History, 1680–1850* (London, 1981).

8. J. De Vries, *European Urbanization, 1500–1800* (London, 1984), esp. pp. 199–249.

9. R.B. Sheridan, *The School for Scandal* (1777): Epilogue, spoken by Lady Teazle.

10. A. Pope, 'Epistle to Miss Blount, on her Leaving the Town, after the Coronation' (1717) in *The Poems of Alexander Pope*, ed. J. Butt, (Oxford, 1975), p. 243.

11. B. Hill (ed.), *Eighteenth-Century Women: An Anthology* (London, 1984), pp. 38–43, 229–44.

12. Smollett, *Humphry Clinker*, p. 100. For an introduction to the immense literature on eighteenth-century London, see G. Rudé, *Hanoverian London, 1714–1808* (London, 1971) and sources cited there.

13. Compare L. Simond, *An American in Regency England: The Journal of a Tour in 1810-11*, ed. C. Hibbert (London, 1968), p. 26; with B. Disraeli *Coningsby: Or, the New Generation* (1844); ed. S.M. Smith (Oxford, 1982), pp. 143, 101 ('the Age of Ruins is past').

14. W. Godwin, *Things as they Are: Or, the Adventures of Caleb Williams* (1794), ed. D. McCracken (Oxford, 1977), p. 254.

15. J. Addison in *The Spectator*, no. 131, 31 July 1711.

16. P.J. Corfield, *The Impact of English Towns, 1700–1800* (Oxford, 1982), pp. 1–16, gives figures and maps of English urbanisation to 1801.

17. A. Smith, *An Inquiry into the Nature and Causes of the Wealth of Nations* (1776), Book III, chapter IV.

18. As well as Rudé (above n. 12), see the classic study by M.D. George, *London Life in the Eighteenth Century* (1925; paperback reissue 1966); and challenging interpretation in M. Byrd, *London Transformed: Images of the City in the Eighteenth Century* (New Haven and London, 1978).

19. There are local studies, of varying quality, of most English urban centres in the eighteenth century, and much new research is currently in progress. Excellent studies by R.G. Wilson, *Gentlemen Merchants: The Merchant Community in Leeds, 1700–1830* (Manchester, 1971); G. Jackson, *Hull in the Eighteenth Century: A Study in Economic and Social History* (Oxford, 1972); and J.W.F. Hill, *Georgian Lincoln* (Cambridge, 1966), provide insights into contrasting urban communities.

20. Corfield, *Impact*, pp. 42–3 (Whitehaven), and 51–65 (resorts). See also J.K. Walton, *The English Seaside Resort: A Social History, 1750–1914* (Leicester, 1983).

21. Fascinating material has been reprinted in the following works: R. Palmer (ed.), *A Touch on the Times: Songs of Social Change,*

1770–1914 (Harmondsworth, 1974) and J. Holloway and J. Black (eds), *Later English Broadside Ballads*, 2 vols (London, 1975, 1979).

22. J.D. Chambers, 'Population change in a provincial town: Nottingham, 1700–1800' in L.S. Pressnell (ed.), *Studies in the Industrial Revolution* (London, 1960).

23. For general context, see Corfield, *Impact*, pp. 168–85; for Sydney Smith's strictures upon Edinburgh streets, see A. Bell, *Sydney Smith* (Oxford, 1980), pp. 14–16.

24. There are major controversies between historians as to the extent and significance of change in eighteenth-century England. For two views, contrasting both in tone and content, see R. Porter, *English Society in the Eighteenth Century* (Pelican Social History of Britain, 1982); and J.C.D. Clark, *English Society, 1688–1832: Ideology, Social Structure, and Political Practice during the Ancien Regime* (Cambridge, 1985).

25. From 'Auguries of Innocence' (c. 1803–4) in W. Blake, *The Poems of William Blake*, ed. W.H. Stevenson (London, 1972), p. 588.

26. H. Walpole to George Montagu, in W.S. Lewis (ed.), *Horace Walpole's Correspondence, Vol. IX* (New Haven, Mass., 1941), p. 386.

5. The Working Classroom *Philip Gardner*

1. *1851 Population Census*, PRO HO 107/1949.
2. Parliamentary Papers (PP) 1861, XXI, *Newcastle Commission*, vol. 2, p. 262.
3. G.C.T. Bartley, *The Schools for the People* (London, 1871), p. 19.
4. Bristol School Board, *Review of Proceedings* (Bristol, 1875), p. 6.
5. See *The Times*, 30 Jan. 1875, p. 1. Surviving memorials are in PRO Ed. 10/11.
6. PP 1878, LX, '*Circular to Her Majesty's Inspectors*', 16 Jan. 1878.
7. *Newcastle*, vol. 2, p. 36.
8. Thomas Cooper, *The Life of Thomas Cooper Written by Himself* (1872), p. 7.
9. 'A Condemned Institution' in *Good Words* (Edinburgh, 1873), p. 746.
10. 'Statistical Inquiries into the Social Condition of the Working Classes, and into the Means Provided for the Education of their Children' in *Central Society for Education. Second Publication* (1838), p. 254.
11. *Committee of Council on Education. Minutes* (1876–7), p. 565.
12. PP 1870, LIV, *Schools for the Poorer Classes. Special Reports*, p. 107.
13. 'An Old Potter' (Charles Shaw), *When I Was a Child* (1903), p. 1.
14. P.H. Fisher, *Notes and Recollections of Stroud, Gloucs.* (1871), p. 291.
15. Bartley, *Schools for the People*, p. 404.
16. *1861 Population Census*, PRO RG 9/1712.
17. *1871 Population Census* PRO RG 10/2505.
18. *Newcastle*, vol. 2, p. 336.
19. PP 1851, XXIII, *Reports from Inspectors of Factories*, p. 55.
20. PP 1837–8, VII, *Select Committee on the Education of the Poorer Classes*, p. 77.

21. N. Senior, *Suggestions on Popular Education* (1861), p. 29.
22. *Newcastle*, vol. 2, pp. 224–5.
23. PP 1843, XIV, *Children's Employment Commission*, p. e3.

6. **Domestic Harmony, Public Virtue** *Catherine Hall*

1. There is a fairly extensive literature on the Queen Caroline affair, much of which focuses on the activities of the radicals. For an interesting recent account see T.W. Lacqueur, 'The Queen Caroline affair: politics as art in the reign of George IV', *J. Modern History*, no. 54, (Sept. 1982). It is also discussed in L. Davidoff and C. Hall, *Family Fortunes: Men and Women of the English Middle Class 1780–1850* (London, 1987), which deals at length with most of the issues touched on in this article.
2. On the growth of the reading public see R.D. Altick, *The English Common Reader* (Chicago, 1963).
3. Anon., *The King's treatment of the Queen, shortly stated to the people of England* (London, 1820). There is an extensive collection in the British Library of pamphlets, broadsheets and songs stemming from the affair.
4. Anon., *Queen Caroline*, British Library Mss. Coll.
5. Anon., *Ode to George the IV and Caroline his wife*, British Library Mss. Coll.
6. On the older aristocratic code see L. Stone, *The Family, Sex and Marriage in England 1500–1800* (London, 1977).
7. See, for example, C. Hill, *Society and Puritanism in Pre-Revolutionary England* (London, 1964).
8. C. Hall, 'The early formation of Victorian domestic ideology' in S. Burman (ed.), *Fit Work for Women* (London, 1979).
9. M.G. Jones, *Hannah More 1745–1833* (Cambridge, 1952).
10. H. More, *Coelebs in search of a wife comprehending of domestic habits and manners, religion and morals*, 2 vols, 9th edn (London, 1809), vol. 2, p. 173.
11. There is a substantial literature on the Evangelicals. The most helpful introduction is I. Bradley, *The Call to Seriousness: the Evangelical Impact on the Victorians* (London, 1976).
12. For a detailed account of the exclusion of women from the pits see A. John, *By the Sweat of their Brow. Women Workers at Victorian Coal Mines* (London, 1984).
13. L. Davidoff and C. Hall, 'The architecture of public and private life: English middle-class society in a provincial town 1780–1850' in D. Fraser and A. Sutcliffe (eds), *the Pursuit of Urban History* (London, 1983).
14. I. Pinchbeck, *Women Workers and the Industrial Revolution 1750–1850* (London, 1981).
15. J. Luckcock, *Moral Culture* (Birmingham, 1817), *Sequel to Memoirs in Humble Life* (Birmingham 1825), 'On the contemplated representation

of Birmingham' (Birmingham, 1827).

16. Luckcock, *Sequel.*

17. On the development of Edgbaston see D. Cannadine, *Lords and Landlords: The Aristocracy and the Towns 1774–1967* (Leicester, 1980).

18. J. Luckcock, 'My house and garden; Lime Grove Edgbaston', Birmingham reference Library Mss. Coll. 375948.

19. The phrase comes in a letter from a West Midlands travelling salesman to his wife. Shaw Letters. Birmingham University Library Mss. Coll. Letter No. 21.

20. For an extended discussion of the farm see L. Davidoff, 'The role of gender in the first industrial nation: agriculture in England 1780–1850', in R. Crompton and M. Mann (eds), *Gender and Stratification* (Cambridge, 1986).

21. Announcements of sales in newspapers are a helpful source on furnishing. For advice to the middle class as to how to build and furnish their homes and design their gardens see J.C. Loudon's many works, especially *The Suburban Gardener and Villa companion: comprising the choice of a suburban or villa residence, or of a situation on which to form one: the arrangement and furnishing of the house; and the laying out, planting general management of the garden, and grounds, especially intended for those who know little re gardening and ladies* (London 1838).

22. W. Cobbett, *Rural Rides* (Harmondsworth, 1967), *Cottage Economy* (London, 1822); S. Bamford, *Passages in the Life of a Radical* (Oxford, 1967).

23. K.D.M. Snell, *Annals of the Labouring Poor. Social Change and Agrarian England 1660–1900* (Cambridge, 1985).

24. H. Land, 'The family wage' in *Feminist Review* no. 6 (1980).

7. The Victorian State: Order or Liberty? *V.A.C. Gatrell*

1. The theme of this chapter is developed more fully in V.A.C. Gatrell, 'Crime, authority and the policeman-state, 1750-1950', in F.M.L. Thompson (ed.), *The Cambridge Social History of Britain, 1750–1950* 3 vols (Cambridge, 1988).

2. V.A.C. Gatrell and T.B. Hadden, 'Nineteenth-century criminal statistics and their interpretation', in E.A. Wrigley (ed.), *Nineteenth-century Society: Essays in the Use of Quantitative Methods for the Study of Social Data* (Cambridge, 1972).

3. Anon., 'Causes of the increase of crime', *Blackwood's Edinburgh Magazine*, LVI (1844).

4. For a general survey, see J.A. Sharpe, *Crime in Early Modern England, 1550–1750* (London, 1984).

5. *Report of the Royal Commission on the County Constabulary,* Parliamentary Papers, 1839 [169], XIX pp. 184–5.

6. General surveys of nineteenth-century policing abound. A good introduction is C. Emsley, *Policing and its Context, 1750–1950* (London, 1983). See also: D. Philips, '"A new engine of power and authority": the institutionalisation of law-enforcement in England, 1780–1830', in V.A.C. Gatrell, B. Lenman and G. Parker (eds), *Crime and the Law: the Social History of Crime in Western Europe since 1500* (London, 1980); W.R. Miller, *Cops and Bobbies: Police Authority in New York and London, 1830–1870* (Chicago and London, 1977); C. Steedman, *Policing the Victorian Community: the Formation of English Provincial Police Forces, 1856–1870* (London, 1984). Semi-official police histories are useful if uncritical and self-congratulatory: T.A. Critchley, *A History of Police in England and Wales, 1900–1966* (London, 1967); and D. Ascoli, *The Queen's Peace: the Metropolitan Police, 1829–1979* (London, 1979).

7. Ascoli, *The Queen's Peace*, provides a convenient guide to these and like developments.

8. V.A.C. Gatrell, 'The decline of theft and violence in Victorian and Edwardian England', in Gatrell, Lenman and Parker (eds), *Crime and the Law*, p. 275.

9. J. Pellew, *The Home Office, 1848–1914: from Clerks to Bureaucrats* (London, 1982).

10. Gatrell, 'The decline of theft and violence'; for assaults on police see PRO, Mepo. 2/752.

11. J.F. Stephen, *A General View of the Criminal Law of England* (London, 1863), pp. 99–100, quoted by D. Hay, 'The criminal prosecution in England and its historians', *Modern Law Review*, 47:1 [1984], 28.

12. See P. Smith, *Disraelian Conservatism and Social Reform* (London, 1967), p. 162; *Pall Mall Gazette*, 26 Aug. 1872; J. Butler, *Government by Police* (1879), p. 56. I owe these references and those in the next footnote to Stefan Petrow.

13. S. Amos, *Fifty years of the English Constitution, 1830–1880* (London, 1880); R. Muir, *Peers and Bureaucrats* (1910), pp. 5–8.

14. The following discussion draws on Gatrell, 'The decline of theft and violence' and 'Crime, authority and the policeman-state'.

15. J. Davis, 'The London garotting panic of 1862: a moral panic and the creation of a criminal class in mid-Victorian England', in Gatrell, Lenman and Parker (eds), *Crime and the Law*.

16. PRO: HO 45: 10595/18736; 9673/A46696B; 9605/A1842B; 9788/B3845A; 10636/202756.

17. Report of the Departmental Committee on Prisons, Parliamentary Papers, 1895, LVI, pp. 9–12.

18. Sir R. Anderson, articles in *Nineteenth Century* (1901), reprinted in his *Criminals and Crime: some Facts and Suggestions* (London, 1907).

19. L. Radzinowicz and R. Hood, 'Incapacitating the habitual criminal: the English experience', *Michigan Law Review*, 78:8 (1980), 1305–89.

8. A Union without Unity *Roy Foster*

1. T. Moore, *The Memoirs of Captain Rock* (published anonymously, Dublin, 1824).
2. The best survey is still Maurice Craig, *Dublin 1660–1860* (Dublin, 1969); see also relevant chapters of T.W. Moody and W.E. Vaughan (eds), *A New History of Ireland, vol IV: 1691–1800* (Oxford, 1986).
3. L.M. Cullen, *An Economic History of Ireland since 1600* (London, 1972), chs 3–4, and *The Emergence of Modern Ireland 1600–1900* (London, 1981), provide a good introduction.
4. With the advent of the Rockingham group to power, promises made to the Irish opposition had to be called to account.
5. For Tone, and the French connection generally, the definitive work is Marianne Elliott, *Partners in Revolution: the United Irishmen and France* (London, 1982).
6. Further expeditions followed, including Humbert's famous foray into Mayo which established the temporary 'Republic of Connacht' in 1798, and the small force which was captured off Lough Swilly in October of the same year. Wolfe Tone was on board, and later committed suicide in prison.
7. Such as Caravats, Shanavests, Terry Alts, Whitefeet, Rockites, etc. (The generic term 'Ribbonmen' was sometimes applied, but technically belongs to a more politicised movement.) Moore's satirical *Captain Rock*, quoted above, is a commentary on Irish grievances which purports to be a family history of the leader of one such group.
8. See *Phineas Finn, The Irish Member* (1869), *Phineas Redux* (1873); also the more obviously 'Irish' *The Kellys and the O'Kellys* (1848) and *The MacDermots of Ballycloran* (1847). Trollope lived in Ireland for some years as a post-office surveyor, and is in many ways a more accurate observer than – for instance – Thackeray.
9. The best treatment is Fergus O'Ferrall, *Catholic Emancipation: Daniel O'Connell and the birth of Irish democracy* (Dublin, 1985).
10. The culmination was his own return for Co. Clare in 1828, which raised the spectre of a secessionist parliament of democratically but illegitimately elected Irish MPs. This tactic, never put into practice by O'Connell, was later threatened by Parnell and finally adopted by Sinn Féin after their landslide victory in the 1918 election.
11. See the popular nationalist histories published as *The Library of Ireland*; also Thomas Davis's very popular poetry, notably 'A Nation Once Again'.
12. Notably the group centred around the *Dublin University Magazine*, which included Isaac Butt, later founder of the Home Government Association from which the Home Rule movement evolved.
13. See D. Kerr, *Peel, Priests and Politics: Sir Robert Peel's administration and the Roman Catholic Church in Ireland 1841–1846* (Oxford, 1982).
14. Called the Royal Irish Constabulary from 1867.

15. The issue upon which Peel nearly separated from his more conservative followers.

16. See, for theories about the Irish problem, R.D.C. Black, *Economic Thought and the Irish Question 1817–1870* (Cambridge, 1960); and for a stimulating analysis, Raymond Crotty, *Irish Agricultural Production: its Volume and Structure* (Cork, 1966), chs 1–3.

17. This analysis, first pioneered by K.H. Connell, has been questioned and adapted in a vast and growing literature, but the basic connection between population growth, early marriages and the potato economy (not simply the potato diet) has not really been refuted.

18. Over a million emigrated between 1815 and 1845, before any signs of national potato famine. See D. Fitzpatrick, *Irish Emigration 1801–1921* (Studies in Irish Economic and Social History, Dublin, 1984).

19. Irish was spoken by about half the population in 1800, but by 1851 only 5 per cent of the population was exclusively Irish-speaking and less than a quarter spoke it at all.

20. See his *Jail Journal*, originally published in 1854, and often reprinted.

21. See R.V. Comerford, *The Fenians in Context* (Dublin, 1984).

22. Which he had disestablished in 1869, though on rather advantageous terms.

9. The View from the Colonies *David Dabydeen*

1. G.S. Graham, *A Concise History of the British Empire* (London, 1970), p. 40.

2. Ibid.

3. A.E. Smith, *Colonists in Bondage* (Gloucester, Mass., 1965), p. 313.

4. Ibid., p. 117.

5. Werner Schlote, *British Overseas Trade from 1700 to the 1930s* (Oxford, 1952) contains a wealth of statistical information on British colonial trade. See also Ralph Davis, *The Industrial Revolution and British Overseas Trade* (Leicester, 1979).

6. Cited in Patrick Richardson, *Empire and Slavery* (London, 1968), p. 9.

7. For an exhaustive statistical account of slavery, see P.D. Curtin, *The Atlantic Slave Trade. A Census* (Madison and London, 1969).

8. Cited in Eric Williams, *Capitalism and Slavery* (London, 1964), p. 51.

9. Cited in David Dabydeen (ed.), *The Black Presence in English Literature* (Manchester, 1985), p. 29.

10. Cited in David Dabydeen, *Hogarth's Blacks. Images of Blacks in Eighteenth Century Art* (London and Aarhus, 1985), p. 30.

11. Cited in Peter Fryer's *Staying Power. The History of Black People in Britain* (London, 1984), p. 154.

12. Ibid., p. 128.

13. Williams, *Capitalism and Slavery*, p. 36.

14. Fryer, *Staying Power*, p. 57.

15. Williams, *Capitalism and Slavery*, pp. 101, 104.

16. Ibid., p. 102.
17. Cited in D.R. Headrick, *The Tools of Empire* (Oxford, 1981), p. 17.
18. See Bernard Porter, *The Lion's Share. A Short History of British Imperialism 1850–1983* (London 1984).
19. See Fryer, *Staying Power*, for short biographies of Davidson and other black radicals of the period.
20. P. Fryer, *Staying Power*, p. 241.
21. Ibid., p. 246.
22. Cited in P. Edwards and J. Walvin, *Black Personalities in the Era of the Slave Trade* (London, 1983), p. 90.
23. A modern paperback edition, edited by Paul Edwards, was published by Heinemann in 1967.
24. Cited in Fryer, *Staying Power*, p. 480.

10. A Week at the Seaside *James Walvin*

1. On the history of sports see W.J. Baker, *Sports in the Western World* (Totowa, N.J., 1982).
2. J.A. Mangan and J. Walvin (eds), *Manliness and Morality* (Manchester, 1987).
3. Hugh Cunningham, 'Leisure', in John Benson (ed.), *The Working Class in England, 1875–1914* (London, 1985).
4. S. Coit and J.A. Hobson (eds), *The Ethical World*, III, No. 16 (April 1900).
5. Quoted in James Walvin, *The People's Game. A Social History of British Football* (London, 1975), pp. 66, 77.
6. Quoted in James Walvin, *Beside the Seaside. A Social History of the Popular Seaside Holiday* (London, 1978), p. 16.
7. Hugh Cunningham, *Leisure in the Industrial Revolution* (London, 1980).
8. R.W. Malcolmson, *Popular Recreations in English Society, 1700–1850* (Cambridge, 1973).
9. J.A.R. Pimlott, *The Englishman's Holiday: A Social History* (London, 1947; repr. Brighton, 1976); J.K. Walton, *The English Seaside Resort, A Social History, 1750–1914* (Leicester, 1983).
10. On railways, see Walton, *English Seaside Resort*.
11. Quoted in Walvin, *Beside the Seaside*, pp. 38, 39.
12. On 'zoning', see H.J. Perkin, 'The "social tone" of Victorian seaside resorts in the north-west', *Northern History*, XI (1976 for 1975), 180–94.
13. Walton, *English Seaside Resort*.
14. For the rise of consumerism see ibid, ch. 2.
15. James Walvin, *A Child's World. A Social History of English Childhood* (London, 1982).
16. F.B. Smith, *The People's Health, 1830–1910* (London, 1979).
17. Walton, *English Seaside Resort*, ch. 7.

11. The Leap in the Dark *Michael Bentley*

1. The classical text is, of course, Edmund Burke's *Reflexions on the Revolution in France* (1790). For modern treatments of the impact of the French Revolution on Britain, see Clive Emsley, *British Society and the French Wars 1793–1815* (London 1979) and Albert Goodwin, *The Friends of Liberty: the English democratic revolution in the age of the French Revolution* (1979).
2. The Reform Act and its consequences are helpfully discussed in Michael Brock, *The Great Reform Act* (London, 1973) and Norman Gash, *Politics in the Age of Peel* (London, 1953, 1966).
3. Greville's diary, 1 April 1832, in Henry Reeve (ed.), *The Greville Memoirs: a journal of the reigns of King George IV and King William IV* (3 vols, 1875), II, 280; Croker to Lord Hertford, 28 Feb. 1832, in Louis J. Jennings (ed.), *The Correspondence and Diaries of the late Rt. Hon. John Wilson Croker* (3 vols, 1884), II, 152.
4. Benjamin Disraeli, *Lothair* (1875), XI.
5. These developments are examined from a Marxist standpoint in E.P. Thompson, *The Making of the English Working Class* (London, 1963).
6. See Eric Hobsbawm, 'The labour aristocracy in nineteenth-century Britain', in *Labouring Men: studies in the history of labour* (London, 1964); and A.E. Musson, 'Class struggle and the Labour Aristoracy', *Social History* (1976), 335–56.
7. For Lowe's career and contribution to the debate about democracy, see James Winter, *Robert Lowe* (Toronto, 1976).
8. A reader wishing to delve deeper into this issue should consult Robert Stewart, *The Politics of Protection: Lord Derby and the protectionist party 1841–52* (Cambridge, 1971) and Travis L. Crosby, *English Farmers and the Politics of Protection* (Hassocks, 1977).
9. For a good introduction to the politics of the 1850s, see J.B. Conacher, *The Peelites and the Party System 1846–52* (London, 1972) and the same author's *The Aberdeen Coalition* (Cambridge, 1968).
10. Palmerston to Russell, 28 Oct. 1862, quoted in John Prest, *Lord John Russell* (London, 1972), 393.
11. I Samuel, i–ii.
12. The detailed narrative can be explored in Maurice Cowling, *1867: Disraeli, Gladstone and Revolution* (Cambridge, 1967).
13. See, in particular, Royden Harrison, 'The Tenth April of Spencer Walpole', in Harrison, *Before the Socialists: studies in labour and politics* (London and Toronto, 1965), pp.78–135.
14. The electoral consequences of 1867 are comprehensively surveyed in H.J. Hanham, *Elections and Party Management: politics in the time of Disraeli and Gladstone* (Hassocks, 1978).
15. For the background to the development of local democracy, see E.P. Hennock, *Fit and Proper Persons: ideal and reality in nineteenth-century urban government* (1973).

12. The Invention of the Past *Peter J. Bowler*

1. The classic critique of Whig history is H. Butterfield, *The Whig Interpretation of History* (London, 1931).
2. See J.B. Bury, *The Idea of Progress: an Inquiry into its Growth and Origin* (reprinted New York, 1955).
3. Despite its title, Spencer's *Social Statics* (London, 1851) treats the free-enterprise system as a means of ensuring progress. The first volume of his 'Synthetic Philosophy' was *First Principles* (London, 1862). On Spencer's views, see J.D.Y. Peel, *Herbert Spencer: the Evolution of a Sociologist* (London, 1971).
4. On Tylor and Victorian cultural anthropology, see J.W. Burrow, *Evolution and Society: a Study of Victorian Social Thought* (Cambridge, 1966) and N. Mandelbaum, *History, Man and Reason: a study in Nineteenth-Century Thought* (Baltimore and London, 1971), ch. 6.
5. On the development of archaeology, see G. Daniel, *A Hundred and Fifty Years of Archaeology* (London, 1975).
6. See D.K. Grayson, *The Establishment of Human Antiquity* (New York, 1983).
7. The architect of the sequential view of archaeological periods was G. de Mortillet, who made explicit political use of the idea of progress, see M. Hammond, 'Anthropology as a weapon of social combat in late-nineteenth-century France,' *J. History Behavioral Sciences*, XVI (1980) 118–32.
8. Acceptance of the earth's antiquity did, of course, generate controversies, see C.C. Gillispie, *Genesis and Geology* (New York, 1959) and A. Hallam, *Great Geological Controversies* (Oxford, 1983).
9. See W. Buckland, *Reliqiae Diluvianae* (London, 1823).
10. On the history of palaeontology, see M.J.S. Rudwick, *The Meaning of Fossils: Episodes on the History of Paleontology* (New York, 1976).
11. Dickens, *Bleak House*, ch. 1.
12. Tennyson, *In Memoriam*, LVI.
13. On the idea of a progressive sequence in the fossil record see Rudwick, *Meaning of Fossils*, ch. 4 and P.J. Bowler, *Fossils and Progress: Paleontology and the Idea of Progressive Evolution in the Nineteenth Century* (New York, 1976).
14. For an account of the debate over Chambers' *Vestiges*, see Gillispie, *Genesis and Geology*, ch. 6.
15. There is an immense literature on the origin and reception of Darwinism; for a survey see P.J. Bowler, *Evolution: the History of an Idea* (Berkeley, Los Angeles and London, 1984) chs 6–10.
16. The belief that 'social Darwinism' was a dominant aspect of late-nineteenth-century thought was popularised by R. Hofstadter, *Social Darwinism in American Thought* (revised edn, New York, 1959). For a critique more in line with the views expressed here, see R. Bannister, *Social Darwinism, Science and Myth in Anglo American Social Thought* (Philadelphia, 1979).

17. On nineteenth-century race theory, see J.H. Haller, *Outcasts from Evolution: Scientific Attitudes of Racial Inferiority, 1859–1900* (Urbana, Illinois, 1975) and N. Stepan, *The Idea of Race in Science: Great Britain, 1800–1960* (London, 1982).

Notes on Contributors

MICHAEL BENTLEY teaches history at the University of Sheffield. His interests centre on the political and intellectual history of Britain in the nineteenth and twentieth centuries, and his best-known publication in this field is *Policies Without Democracy 1815–1914*, a volume in the Fontana History of England series. A new book about the theory and practice of Liberal politics before the First World War will appear in 1987; thereafter Dr Bentley hopes to write a large-scale study of political thought in Britain between the 1870s and 1920s. His reviews of academic books appear frequently in the press and learned journals.

MAXINE BERG is a Senior Lecturer in Economic History at the University of Warwick. She was born in Canada and graduated from Simon Fraser University before coming to England in 1971. She studied at the University of Sussex, then at Oxford and was a Junior Research Fellow in History at Balliol College from 1974–8. She is currently a research reader of the British Academy. She is the author of *Technology and Toil in Nineteenth Century Britain* (1979), *The Machinery Question and the Making of Political Economy 1815–1848* (1980), *The Age of Manufactures* (1985), and a co-editor of *Manufacture in Town and Country before the Factory*, 1983. She is now studying work and skill in eighteenth-century metal trades, and has broader interests in women's history and radical economics.

PETER BOWLER has taught at universities in Canada, Malaysia and the United Kingdom, and is currently Lecturer in History and Philosophy of Science at The Queen's University of Belfast. He has written several books on the development of evolution theory: *Fossils and Progress* (1976), *The Eclipse of Darwinism* (1983), *Evolution: the History of an Idea* (1984) and *Theories of Human Evolution* (1986). He is now writing a reappraisal of the 'Darwinian Revolution' based on his studies of non-Darwinian evolutionism.

MICHAEL BROERS was born in the United States in 1954 and brought up in

Northern Ireland. He graduated from the University of St Andrews in 1978, and gained his D Phil from Worcester College, where he was a Carnegie Research Scholar. He has taught at Kalamazoo College, Michigan, and at the University of York. Since 1985, he has been a lecturer in the School of History at the University of Leeds. He is the author of several articles on Napoleonic Italy and is preparing a book on the French Revolution in Italy.

PENELOPE J. CORFIELD is the author of *The Impact of English Towns, 1700–1800* as well as numerous articles on English social and economic history. She teaches at the University of London and also for the Yale-in-London British Studies course. An enthusiast for big-city life, she has had experience as an elected borough councillor, which she descibes as 'an essential eye-opener for the urban historian'. Her current research is concerned with patterns and significance of social change in early industrial Britain.

DAVID DABYDEEN, from Guyana, read English at Cambridge and London Universities, writing his doctoral dissertation on eighteenth-century English art and society. His first book, *Slave Song*, a collection of poems, was awarded the Cambridge University Quiller-Couch Prize in 1978 and the Commonwealth Poetry Prize in 1984. His other publications include *The Black Presence in English Literature* (1985) and *Hogarth's Blacks: Images of Blacks in Eighteenth Century English Art* (1985). The latter was awarded a GLC Literature Prize in 1985.

ROY FOSTER is Reader in History at Birkbeck College, University of London. He has written *Charles Stewart Parnell: the man and his family* (1976), *Lord Randolph Churchill: a political life* (1981), and numerous articles on aspects of Irish history. He is currently completing a new *Pelican History of Modern Ireland*.

PHIL GARDNER received his doctorate from the University of Sussex in 1984. His book, *The Lost Elementary Schools of Victorian England* won the 1985 S.C.S.E. Prize for a first-time author. He is currently researching a book on the social history of the teaching profession.

V. A. C. GATRELL is a Fellow and Tutor of Gonville and Caius College, Cambridge, and university lecturer in modern British social and economic history. He has published on the nineteenth-century cotton industry, Robert Owen, and the history of crime and police, and is currently working on the history of sexual crime.

CATHERINE HALL has been teaching history and cultural studies at North East London Polytechnic since 1982. From 1978–82 she worked with Leonore Davidoff on an ESRC-funded project at the University of Essex on the middle-class family and middle-class culture in late-eighteenth- and early nineteenth-century England. This research, based on two local studies of industrialising Birmingham and rural Essex and Suffolk, will be published in 1987 as *Family Fortunes: Men and Women of the English Middle Class 1780–1850*. She is continuing to work in the field of the nineteenth-century family.

BOYD HILTON is the Senior Tutor and a Lecturer in History at Trinity College, Cambridge, where he has been since 1974. Before that he was a Research Lecturer at Christ Church, Oxford. He has written *Corn, Cash, Commerce. The Economic Policies of the Tory Governments 1815–30* (1977) and published several articles on aspects of nineteenth-century British political and intellectual history. *The Age of Atonement. The Impact of Evangelicalism on Social and Economic Thought ca.1780–1870* will be published in 1987, and he is also working on a volume in the projected *New Oxford History of England.*

LESLEY M. SMITH, the editor, studied history at the University of St Andrews and Brasenose College, Oxford, where she was awarded her D Phil in 1980. She has edited (with Geoffrey Parker) *The General Crisis of the Seventeenth Century* (1978) and the first three volumes in the Making of Britain series: *The Dark Ages* (1984), *The Middle Ages* (1985) and *The Age of Expansion* (1986). She now works as an associate producer for London Weekend Television.

JAMES WALVIN is Reader in History at the University of York. He has published widely on modern British social history and in the fields of slavery and the slave trade. Among his recent books are *Football and the Decline of Britain* (1986), *England, Slaves and Freedom 1776–1838* (1986) and *English Urban Life 1776–1851* (1984).

Index

aborigines 162
  in evolution 163
Act of Union 1800 105, 106, 107, 115
Addison, Joseph 57
Address to the People of the United Kingdom
  of Great Britain and Ireland on the threat
  of Invasion (1803) 13
Africa 120, 123
  colonisation 123–4
  football in 131
  life in 128–9
agriculture 4
  capital from 30–1
  decline in 25–6
  flight from 26–7, 53–4, 57, 63
  in Ireland 107, 110–13, 114, 115
America 118–19
American Revolution 10–14
  effects on Britain 13
  effects on France 13
  effects on Ireland 104–5
  French intervention 12–13
  ideology 10, 12–14
  long-term effects 13–14
Anderson, Sir Robert 100
Anti-Corn Law League 148, 149–50
The Anti-Jacobin 20
Anti-Slavery Movement 81
anthropology 162–3
  and biological determinism 169–70
  and Social Darwinism 169
archaeology 162–3
  fossil record 163–5, 166–7
  terminology 162–3
aristocracy: and government 146
Arkwright, Richard 32
Ashley, Lord 82
Atlantic trade 10
atonement 39, 41
Austen, Jane 49
Australia 118, 199, 162

Babylon 50, 51, 59, 61
bag hosiers 33
Bamford, Samuel 30, 35, 86–7

Bank Holidays 132
Barchester 58
Barclays's Bank 123
Barnsley 59
Bartley, George 72
Bath 53, 59, 79, 134
  season in 135
Beer Street 51
Belfast 105, 110
Bewick, Thomas 26
Bible 37, 50
Bill of Pains and Penalties 77
Birmingham 26–8, 31, 49, 57, 58, 78, 84–6,
  123
Blackpool 137, 139, 141–2
Blackwood's Magazines 91
Blake, William 61
Blue Books 64
Bognor Regis 59
Bonaparte, Napoleon 18
  armies 18
  British views of 20
  defeat 19
  victories 18–19
Boulton, Matthew 30
Bournemouth 137
Breughel, Pieter 50
Brierly, Ben 28
Bright, John 152
Brighton 132, 136–7, 138
Bristol 12, 63, 79
  and slave trade 122
  private adventure schools 72–3
  School Board 67
Britain:
  and Ireland 103–15 *passim*
  and slave trade 119–20
  constitution 147, 160–1
  counter-revolutionaries 19–20
  decline 2–3, 24, 25
  democracy 145–57 *passim*
  education 63–74 *passim*
  effects of French Revolution 22
  elections 11, 149
  Empire 7, 11, 117–30 *passim*

Britain – *continued*
   family life   88–8
   ideological reaction to French
         Revolution   20–1
   law and order   89–101 *passim*
   political parties   145, 149–57
   political reaction to French
      Revolution   20
   population growth   24–5
   position after 1815   19, 22
   reaction to American Revolution   13
   reaction to French Revolution   16–22
   rivalry with France   8–22 *passim*
   social policy   44, 61, 66
   stability   44
   town life   49–62 *passim*
   wars with France   16–22
British Navy   12, 18
   mutinies   21
Buckland, William   164–5
Burke, Edmund   13, 15

calico printing   27, 28–9
Calthorpe, Lord   85, 86
Canada   12
capitalism   45–7
carders   27
Carlyle, Thomas   23
Caroline of Brunswick   75–9, 80, 85, 86
   trial of   77–8
Castlereagh, Lord   16, 19
catastrophism   42
Catholics:
   emancipation of   104, 108–10
   in Britain   43, 57
   in Ireland   38, 104
Central Investigation Department:
      introduction of   93–4
Chambers, Robert   167
Charlotte, Princess   76
Chartism   44, 127–8, 148
Chesterfield, Lord   120
childhood   140–1
Children's Employment Commission   82
cholera   43–4, 147
Jesus Christ   39, 41, 47
Church of England   39, 40
   evangelicals in   42, 80–2
   retribution in   39, 41
   theology   41, 42, 43, 47
Churchill, Winston   101
City of London   11
Cobbett, William   86–7
Coelebs in Search of a Wife   81
Condon, William   98, 99
Conservative Party   145
   and reform   154–67
   and working-classes   156–7
   decisions in   150
   governments   150–1
craftsmen   26–7
creation   6, 39
   attitudes to   6, 42, 163–4

crime:
   definition of   90–1, 95–6
   professionalisation of   98–101
   rates   91–2, 99–100
Crimean War   156
criminal records system   98, 100
   introduction   95
criminals   95–6, 98–101
   deportation   118–19
Croker, John Wilson   147
Crompton, Richard   28
Cuffay, William   127–8

Darwin, Charles   42
   and archaeology   166
   and evolution   167–70
   and progress   168
   and social Darwinism   169
Davidson, William   125–6
de Coubertin, Baron   131
Decline and Fall of the Roman Empire   160
democracy   4, 6
   struggle for   145–57 *passim*
Derby, Lord   154
Dickens, Charles   41, 98
   and archaeology   166
dinosaurs   164–5
disciplinary state   89–91, 92, 95, 96, 98
Disraeli, Benjamin   6, 44, 56, 146, 150, 154–7
Druscovitch, Chief Inspector   93

earth: origins of   42–3, 163–5, 166–7,
      169–70
Easter   41
economic growth: mechanisms of   24–5,
      45–6
economic liberalism   23–4
Edgbaston   85–6
Edinburgh   61
education:
   Department of   67
   state provision of   66–7, 68, 73–4
   working class attitudes to   66–74 *passim*
Education Act (1870)   67
Education Act (1876)   67–8
Eldon, Lord   19
electorate   145
   in the cities   156
   increase in   147, 155–7
   size of   146
   women in   157
Elton, Mrs   49
Empire   117–30 *passim*
   and social Darwinism   170
enclosure   25
Equiano, Olaudah   128
   views on British   128–30
Evangelicals   80–2
evolution   42
   industrial society in   162–3
   social   162
   structure of   167–9
Exeter   79

Facey, Mary   72
factory systm   25
Fenianism   114–15
financial institutions   122–3
Fisher, Paul Hawkins   71–2
Fitch, J.G.   71
football   131, 132, 134
France   7, 8–22 *passim*
    civil wars   16
    economy   12
    empire   12
    population   12
    position in Europe   11–12
    revolutionary wars   7
French Revolution   8–22 *passim*, 35, 80,
    146, 159
    and Britain   11–22 *passim*
    defeat   19
    democracy in   14
    events   14
    foreign policy   15
    ideology   10–11, 14–15, 16
    military success   18–19
    propaganda   19–21
    reforms during   15
    resistance to   21

garrotting   99
geology   42
    and history   163–4
George III   75, 77
George IV   75–9, 80
Germany   7
Gibbon, Edward   160
Gillray   20–1
Gin Lane   51
Gladstone, William Ewart   6, 38, 113, 146,
    149, 152, 154–5
Glasgow   33
God   37–8, 41–4, 46, 48, 81
Godwin, William   161
Graham, Sir James   38–9
Grattan, Henry   104
Grey, Earl   147, 149

Habsburg Empire   8
Halifax   79
Hargreaves, James   32
The Harlot's Progress   55
Heaven   39, 41, 42, 47, 48
Hell   39, 42, 47, 48
Hell-upon-Earth   51
History:
    and the Victorians   160–71 *passim*
    Whig interpretation of   160–1
Hitchcock, Anne   63, 64, 72
Hitchcock, Henry   63, 64, 72
Hogarth, William   51, 59
holidays   *see* seaside resorts
Holyoake, George Jacob   27–8
Home Office   93, 94, 95, 96, 99, 100
Hotham, Sir Richard   58
House of Lords   77, 78

Hundred Year's War   8
Hutton, William   27–8, 49, 51, 53, 61

incarnation   41
India   12, 117
    economy of   124
    revolts in   125, 156
Industrial Revolution   4–7, 23–36 *passim*,
    79–80, 159–60
    children in   26–30
    effects on family life   87–8, 91
    entrepreneurs   30, 135, 146
    espionage in   31–2
    finance for   30
    interpretations of   23–5
    labour in   25–6
    mechanisation in   27
    public health during   35–6, 44, 61, 133, 141
    reactions to   34–6, 134
    regional differences in   30–1
    technology in   23, 33–4
    women in   26–7, 35–6
Ireland   7, 103–15 *passim*
    agriculture   110–11
    famine   37–9, 43, 47, 110–14
    Home Rule   114
    migration from   57, 118
    nationalism in   38
    Repeal movement in   108–9
    stereotypes of   107
Ivanhoe   160

Jacobinism:
    agitation for   21
    and politics   16
    in Britain   19–20, 21
    in France   16–17
Jamaica   120, 123
Jars, Gabriel   31
Jerusalem   61
John Bull turned into a galley slave   20
Justices of the Peace   92

Kingsley, Charles   160
knitting industry   32–3
Knox, William   120

Labour Party   156
Lancashire   8, 78
Leeds   26, 58, 78, 79
legal system   4
leisure industry   131, 135–6
Leyland, Thomas   123
Liberal Party   145, 149, 150
    and reform   152–5, 160
Limited Liability Act (1856)   44–6
Liverpool   12, 26
    and slave trade   121–2, 123
London   26, 31, 53, 58, 59, 62, 80
Lowe, Robert   149
Lubbock, John   163
Luckcock, James   86
    biography   84

Lyell, Sir Charles   42, 163

MacCauley, Baron   117, 161–2
McCullock, John   46
Malthus, Robert   43
Manchester   26, 28, 56, 58, 59, 61, 78, 123,
   126
Marryat, Joseph   123
mass media   99–100
Maurice, Frederick, Denison   39, 47–8
Maynooth   38, 43
medicine   44, 46, 61
Meiklejohn, Inspector   93
metal trades   27, 28, 30
middle classes:
   and reform   149
   family life   82–3
   homes   85–6
   leisure   134, 142–3
   patterns of work among   83–5
   religious beliefs   37–48 passim, 80–2
   social investigations of   65
   views on education   65, 73–4
Midland Bank   123
The Mines and Collieries Bill   82
mining   26, 82
Mitchel, John   113
Moore, Thomas   103
More, Hannah   80–1
Morice, Humphrey   122
My House and Garden   86

Nash, Richard 'Beau'   59
Nasmyth, James   23
Neave, Richard   122
New Lanark   33
New Testament   41–2
Newton, John   130
Northamptonshire   28
Northern Star   127–8
Norwich   28, 57
Nottingham   60, 79

O'Connell, Daniel   108–10, 112
Ode to George the Fourth and Caroline His
   Wife   79
Old Bailey   93, 98
Old Testament   42, 163–4
Olympic movement   131
Origin of Species   167, 169
Owen, Richard   164–5, 166
Owen, Robert   33

Paine, Thomas   13, 19–20
Pall Mall Gazette   96
Palmer, Chief Inspector   93
Palmerston, Lord   149, 152
parlement of Paris   11
Parliament   11, 35–6, 43, 99, 130, 151
   Irish loyalty to   107
   Irish representation in   105–6
   radicals in   154–5
   reform of   145–57 passim

Peel, Robert   30, 39, 92–3, 110, 149–51
Percival, Spencer   43
Peterloo massacre   125–6
Pilkington, Hugh   99
Pitt, William (the elder)   18
Pitt, William (the younger)   15–22 passim,
   61, 81, 105, 157
Plymouth   58
police:
   attacks on   96
   corruption in   93–4
   introduction of   92–3
Political Register   87
poor law   26, 44, 148
Pope, Alexander   54
Pope's Parade, Bristol   63, 72
population census   63, 66, 72–3
Porter, G.R.   70
Portsmouth   58
Preston Pilot   137
Prevention of Crime Act (1908)   100–1
providence   37, 44, 46

radicalism   126
   and history   161
   and reform   148, 151–2, 155–6
   and slavery   126–8
railways   137
   and seaside resorts   137–40
Reform Act (1832)   146–7
Reform Act (1867)   146
   passing of   155–6
   prelude to   152–5
   results of   156–7
Reform League   149, 155
revolution   43–4
Rhyll   137
Romantic movement   160
Rountree, Seebohim   3
rural industry   26
   embezzlement in   31
   indebtedness in   32
   putting-out system in   32
rural life   51–3, 54–5, 61
Rural Rides   87
Russel, Dr   136–7, 141
Rusell, Lord John   150, 152

Sandon, Lord   67
Scarborough   137, 138, 139
School for Scandal   54
Scotland Yard   93, 95, 100
Scott, Sir Walter   160
Scourfield, J.H.   96
seaside resorts   132
   and railways   137–8
   and working people   132
   commercialisation of   141–3
   disorder in   143
   growth of   136–7, 138–40
   healthy aspect of   132, 141
   holidays   139
   social division in   138

Second World War   2, 3
Self Help   169
Senior, Nassau   73
Seven Year's War   8, 10
Shaftsbury, Lord   3
Sharp, Granville   120–2
Shaw, Charles   71
Sheffield   23, 26, 58, 59
Sheridan, Oliver   54, 56
Shrewsbury   59
silk trade   28
slaves
    and abolition movement   126–7, 130
    in Britain   125–30
    profits from   122–3
    sale of   129
    trade in   119–20, 121
    transportation of   120–1
    views of   120
Smiles, Samuel   169
Smith, Adam   26, 58
Smollet, Tobias   53
Southend   132
spinners   26, 27, 31
spinning jenny   27, 31, 34–5
spinning mule   34
Staffordshire   28
Stamford   49, 58
steam engines   35–6
Stephen, J.F.   96
Stewart, John   119

technology   4–5
Tennyson, Alfred Lord   166
textile industry   23, 26, 27, 31, 32, 34
theft   89
The Times   99–100
Tone, Wolf   105
Tower of Babel   50
towns: *see also* urbanisation
    administration   61
    attractions   53
    building in   58–9
    effects on economy   57–8
    growth   60–6, 136–7, 138–40
    images   50–1
    migration to   4, 53–4, 57–8, 63–4
    population   57
    problems in   61
    reactions to   55–6, 60–2
    suburban life in   84–7
trade: with colonies   119–20
Trades Union Congress   156
Trevelyan, Sir Charles   38
Troupp, Edward   100
Tyler, Edward B:
    and social Darwinism   169
    news on progress   162

Ulster   105–6
United Irishmen   105
Uphill, Harriet   72
upper classes   53, 61, 97

urbanisation: *see also* towns
    reactions to   50–1
    reasons for   53–4
    results of   62, 63–74 *passim*
    women's role in   54–5

Versailles   12
Victoria   37, 75, 108, 134, 138, 143
Victorian state   2–3, 89–101 *passim, see also*
        Britain
    achievement of   101
    and Ireland   103–15 *passim*
    and prisons   95
    bureaucracy in   96–7
    order in   92
Victorian society   1, *see also* Britain
    and progress   161–2, 167–70
    attitudes to past   159–71
    democracy in   145–57
    family in   5, 75–88, 91
    leisure in   6–7, 131–43
    liberty in   6
    marriage in   79–88
    prosperity of   6, 43
    religious beliefs in   6, 37–48, 163, 166–7
    social change in   6, 65, 91–2, 159–60
    stability of   44
    values of   1–7, 37–48
    women in   78–9, 91

Walpole, Horace   62
Walpole, Spencer   155
War of Austrian Succession   8
War of Polish Succession   8
War of Spanish Succession   8
water-frame   27
Watt, James   123–4
The Wealth of Nations   26, 58
weavers:
    handloom   27, 29
    powerloom   27, 34–5
Wesley, Charles   136
West Indies   120–1, 122, 123, 128
    cricket in   131
    slave revolts in   124
Westminster   7
Westward Ho!   160
Whitby   139
Whitehaven   59
Wilberforce, William   80, 81
Williams-Wynn, Charlotte   47–8
Wood, John   59
Woollen Acts   31
woollen industry   27
working class:
    and drink   132
    and football   133
    and the franchise   152, 153, 156–7
    creation   63–4
    culture   5, 67, 74 *passim*
    family among   81–2, 86–7
    improvement of   65
    historian's view of   66

working class – *continued*
  hostility to   135
  leisure   131, 132, 134–5, 138–9, 143
  problems   64–5
  prosperity   39–41, 148–9, 153–4

Yorkshire   28, 30, 78
Young, Arthur   26
Young Ireland   108–10, 112

Zong (slave ship)   120–1